Perfect Puppy Training

The Complete Guide to Puppy Obedience Training & Puppy Care

MIA MONTAGLIANI

2

Your Dog Needs You is an online resource for dog owners looking for simple and fun dog training tips. The founder of Your Dog Needs You, Mia Montagliani, is a highly sought after dog trainer and is well known for her uncanny ability to empower dog owners to bring the best out from their dogs.

Copyright © 2012 by Mia Montagliani

All rights reserved. With the exception of quoting brief passages for the purposes of review, no part of this publication may be reproduced without prior written permission of the author.

The information in this book is true and complete to the best of the author's knowledge. All recommendations are made without any guarantee on the part of the author, who also disclaims any liability incurred in connection with the use of this material.

The author recognizes that some words, model names, and designations herein are the property of the trademark holder. The author uses them for identification purposes only.

To contact the author, find out about my other publications, or affiliate information, please visit Your Dog Needs You.

ISBN: 978-0-9870561-5-3

Author: Mia Montagliani

Illustrations: Andre Adams
Editor: David Bewster, Clarity in Words
Proof reading: EzyVa

Cover Design: Chris Hayward, Big Map Ideas

Front cover image: iStock.com

Table of Contents

Acknowledgments

I would like to thank my mom and dad, Georgette and Francesco, for always encouraging me to follow my dreams. It takes wise parents to know the difference between what is best for them and what is best for their children.

Thanks to all the owners and their dogs I have trained for allowing me to refine my craft – because of what I have learned from you, I was able to make this an invaluable resource for others.

I would like to thank all the precious dogs I have had the privilege of owning throughout my life. You all taught me much more than I could ever teach you: unconditional love, loyalty and trust. My gratitude knows no bounds – you are all in my heart.

Introduction

Dear puppy owner,

Congratulations on buying *Perfect Puppy Training: The Complete Guide to Puppy Obedience Training and Puppy Care.*

My name is Mia Montagliani and I am the dog trainer at Your Dog Needs You, the premier online resource for dog owners. I help owners train and care for their canine companions humanely, effectively and without stress.

As a dog trainer I get heaps of questions from dog owners about issues relating to their dog's general welfare, ranging from car safety, obedience, insurance to dietary tips, etc. Often these dog owners could not find all the answers they were looking for in one complete resource. Many dog owners like you would say to me: "If only puppies came with a manual!" Well, you spoke –I listened! I developed this guide so puppy owners around the world can own a complete resource dedicated to dog health, training and wellbeing.

This guide is designed to equip you – the new puppy owner – with the right tools and techniques to give complete care and training to your dog. This guide will therefore help you save hundreds off your pet bills because I'll share the latest in basic canine home care, obedience and grooming *plus much more.*

Again, I congratulate you on buying this guide and I trust you and your precious puppy will benefit from it.

Regards,

Mia

Mia Montagliani

READ THIS FIRST

Would you like access to the companion video for this guide?

For your free video on *3 Ways to Motivate Your Dog* go to http://yourdogneedsyou.com/free-stuff and register.

Please REVIEW this book on Amazon.

I want your feedback to make the next version much better.

Thank you so much!

What's Inside This Guide

So you have a new puppy…and you're wondering if this guide is for you.

I wrote this guide with the new puppy owner in mind. This guide is for people wanting to give their puppy the best start to life. But this guide is more than just a 'puppy manual', it's a comprehensive resource that you can refer to over and over again throughout your dog's whole life.

I have also included illustrations that make it easy to follow my training and health care tips. Here's a taste of what you'll discover inside:

How to prepare for your puppy's life

- How to prepare your home environment for your puppy.
- A checklist of what you can do when you bring your puppy home.
- The right equipment for training and caring for your puppy.

Feeding your puppy

The right diet and feeding schedules for puppies.

- The correct amount to feed your dog throughout every stage of life.
- How to prevent food aggression.
- Different diets available for dogs, such as raw, commercial and dry food.
- How to tell the difference between nutritious and dodgy food when reading the labels on packaging.
- Tips on overcoming fussy eating habits.
- Which 20 'human' foods and other materials are very bad for dogs.

Grooming and hygiene

- How to prevent ear infections by keeping your puppy's ears clean and dry.
- How to clip your dog's nails safely, without fuss.
- Simple ways to keep your dog's teeth clean and her breath fresh.
- How to keep your dog's eyes clean and what to do about common eye, lash and lid complaints.
- How to care for different types of coats and which brushes and combs are suitable.
- The safe and hassle-free way to bathe your dog.

Fun, games, children and staving off boredom

- How to ensure your dog is confident, happy and occupied.
- How to exercise your dog, depending on her breed.
- Fun games and toys that will stimulate your dog and excite her curiosity.

Travel

- Ways to ensure car rides are comfortable and safe for you and your dog.
- How to manage car sickness.
- How to manage domestic and international air travel for your dog.

Children and dogs

- How to keep children safe around dogs.
- How to teach children to avoid dog attacks.
- Ways to ensure children treat your puppy nicely.
- Ways you can get your puppy used to children.

Training

- Easy potty training.
- Rate your dog's trainability.

- Basic ground rules professional dog trainers use to makes training easier.
- How to make sure your puppy is eager to learn new commands.
- How to stop bad behavior without hollering, hitting or hurting your puppy.
- How to teach your dog to stand, sit, drop, heel and come.
- How to build your dog's confidence and ensure she is calm around people.
- How to ensure your puppy accepts strange noises, like lawn mowers, vacuum cleaners and vehicles.
- How to stop your puppy chewing your furniture and clothes.
- How to stop your puppy from nipping and biting people's hands and feet.
- How to stop your puppy from peeing herself, jumping or going crazy when she meets people.
- How to train your puppy to be self-sufficient so she won't fret and howl in your absence.

Health and safety

- Important vaccinations.
- Worms, heartworm and fleas.
- Pet insurance.
- What to do if your dog stops breathing or is vomiting.
- What to do if your dog is bleeding, or has been run over by a vehicle or been in a fight.
- What to do if your dog is bitten by a snake.
- What to do if your dog is dry-retching or vomiting.
- How to bandage your dog's ear, tail or leg.
- Which 20 poisonous foods to avoid.
- What to do if your dog has eaten poison.
- What to do if your dog has eaten chocolate.
- What to pack in your dog's first aid and evacuation kits.
- How to handle your dog's heat stroke or heat exhaustion.

- How to give your dog a pill.
- The tell-tale signs of shock and how to manage a dog in shock.

As you can see, this guide is jam-packed full of instructions and tips.

Enjoy your puppy and I hope you have many fun-filled years together!

Chapter 1
How You Can Welcome Your Awesome New Puppy into Your Life

Your puppy's first days are really important; you'll never get another opportunity to give your new dog a warm welcome. The best way to give your puppy the best introduction is to prepare for this occasion.

In this chapter, I'll explain:

- How to ensure that your puppy is the right match for you and your family's lifestyle.
- How to choose a friendly and compliant dog.
- What's involved in adopting a puppy from a shelter or city pound.
- How to prepare your home environment for your new puppy.
- What you can do in the first 24 hours after bringing your puppy home - a checklist is included.
- The right equipment for training and caring for your puppy.
- What to consider when budgeting for your puppy's needs throughout her life.

Choosing the Right Breed - Lifestyle Match Survey

Before you choose your next dog it is important to consider many things, including your lifestyle. Many dogs are surrendered to animal shelters each year because people get a dog on impulse without considering whether the dog will fit in with how they live.

Here are some questions for you to ask yourself before you get your next dog:

1. What kind of residence do you live in?
   ☐ Flat or Apartment
   ☐ Townhouse or Villa or Unit
   ☐ House

The type of your residence is very important in determining what kind of dog is suitable in terms of its size, tendency to bark, and activity level. For example, many small dogs do very well in a flat or apartment and they are popular for this reason. Dogs such as Bichon Frises and Toy Poodles make excellent apartment dogs and can do well in a townhouse. If you live in a house with a yard you may have more options since you can accommodate larger dogs which enjoy more daily exercise. A Golden Retriever or an Irish Setter will love living in a house with a yard.

2. What type of area do you live in?
   ☐ Inner city
   ☐ Suburban
   ☐ Rural

This question is important to ask yourself because some dogs are more suited to living in the city than others. If you live in the city and you must walk your dog every day then you will do well with a small dog such as a Dachshund or a Miniature Schnauzer. These breeds can also do well in the suburbs. Many medium-sized dogs are able to live in the suburbs as long as you have a fenced yard. Good examples include English Springer

Spaniels, Labrador Retrievers, and many terrier breeds. Rural life is ideal for larger dogs that need plenty of exercise on a regular basis. German Shorthaired Pointers, Border Collies and other breeds with high energy levels do well when they have room to run.

However, don't be too discouraged if you love a breed and you don't have the ideal set-up for them. If you are devoted to caring and exercising your dog you can make many situations work. For example, there are many large dogs living in cities that are quite happy as long as their owners take them for a run on a regular basis. Plus, some large dogs are happy with a big morning run after which they prefer to sleep the rest of the day. Many Greyhounds are couch potatoes in an apartment setting as long as they have a good run.

3. What size is the yard in which the dog will live?
   ☐ None
   ☐ Small
   ☐ Medium
   ☐ Large

You should consider what kind of yard you have and how you will meet the exercise needs of any dog you are considering. However, just because you have a large yard does not mean that a dog will self-exercise. Many dogs are quite lazy when left to their own devices. If you want to make sure a dog is getting plenty of exercise, it's always a good idea to do things with your dog. Walks, taking your dog for runs, playing games that require running and exercise, and other kinds of exercise will provide your dog with more exercise than just turning her loose in a big yard.

That's not to say that dogs do not appreciate having a yard. They do. A yard appropriate for your dog's size and level of play is always welcome.

4. Do you have other pets?
   ☐ None
   ☐ Yes – Cat/s
   ☐ Yes – Dog/s
   ☐ Yes – Cat/s and Dog/s

Depending on the individual dog, this question can be very important. Some dogs prefer to be single pets and have all of your attention. On the other hand, some dogs do enjoy having another dog or cat as a playmate. Some dogs get along well with cats and some don't. If you are a cat owner and thinking of getting a terrier breed or a sighthound, however, you will need to take special care that the dog gets along well with cats as these breeds may see their feline 'companion' as prey.

5. What is the gender of your other dogs?
   ☐ Not applicable
   ☐ Female
   ☐ Male
   ☐ Both

If you have other dogs you will need to consider gender roles before you get a new dog. For example, if you have a male, will he get along with another male or see him as a rival? If you have a female, will she fight or flirt with a male? How will your male or female react to bringing in a female dog? You may be setting up a situation where the dogs will fight among themselves by bringing in a new dog. It may make difference if your current dog or the one you are considering is spayed or neutered. The new dog's age may also make a difference. Consider all of these factors before bringing in a new dog. You will be making an enormous change to the life of your current dog and possibly making her or her feel very insecure.

6. Are you able to keep your dog secure?
   ☐Yes
   ☐No
   ☐Sometimes

Before you bring a dog home you will need to be certain that you are able to keep your dog properly confined at all times. A dog that escapes may be hurt or injured. She may cause harm to others — animals or people. She may get into trash or other things in the neighborhood. If she is a nuisance, she could end up at the pound. Some breeds, such as terriers, are particularly prone to digging under fences. Some of the larger hounds have a tendency to climb or jump. Make sure that you can keep a dog safely at home before you get one.

    7. How much time will you spend exercising your dog each day?
- ☐ None
- ☐ 30 minutes
- ☐ 60 minutes
- ☐ More than 60 minutes

Your dog's exercise needs are very important. Before getting any dog you should determine how much time you can spend exercising your dog each day or each week. This will help you choose what kind of dog to get. If you have no time to exercise a dog then it's not a good idea to get a dog that requires an hour of exercise per day. Your dog will be desperately unhappy when she doesn't get enough exercise. The result will be a dog that destroys your home. She will chew, howl, have accidents in the house and be completely unmanageable. And it will not be her fault: her needs are not being met.

8. How active is the owner?
- ☐ Inactive
- ☐ Not very active
- ☐ Quite Active
- ☐ Very Active

Before getting a dog you should consider how active you are. It's best to try to get a dog whose activity level will match your own. This isn't always a matter of size. There are many large dogs, such as some of the mastiff breeds, which are quite content to be quiet and inactive. Some breeds will match their activity level to yours. But if you are a fairly inactive person you should avoid breeds that are known for being very active.

9. Are you experienced at handling or training dogs?
- ☐ No
- ☐ Yes – a little
- ☐ Yes –very

When choosing a dog it's important to be honest with yourself about how experienced you are at handling or training dogs. Some dogs require more training than others to be good pets. Many dogs coming from shelters may have some 'baggage' and will need some extra training to overcome behavior problems. Other dogs can be very easy to train and want very much to please you. Still other dogs can be shy or lack confidence and require a very confident trainer. It's important to match the dog with the right trainer. So, be honest about how much experience you have with dogs and don't take on a dog that needs a lot of work if you haven't had much experience with dogs.

10. How long will your dog be alone each week?
- ☐ Not at all
- ☐ Up to 20 hours
- ☐ 20-40 hours
- ☐ More than 40 hours

This question is very important since dogs behave differently. Some dogs get along fine spending time by themselves, but most dogs prefer to spend more time with their owner or with someone in the house. Consider carefully how much time your dog will be spending alone before you get one. Too much time alone could make your dog develop some behavior problems. Every dog needs quality time with her human family.

11. Do elderly or disabled people stay with you?
    ☐ No
    ☐ Sometimes
    ☐ Often
    ☐ Permanently

Before choosing your next dog you need to consider whether elderly or disabled people stay with you or visit often. Some breeds can be very boisterous and are not well-suited to being around the elderly or disabled. There are many breeds, however, which do very well with older people or people with disabilities.

12. How old is the dog's primary caregiver?
    ☐ 5-18 years old
    ☐ 19-39 years old
    ☐ 40-59 years old
    ☐ Over 60 years old

Before getting a dog you should consider who the dog's primary caregiver will be. Some dogs can be very hard for a young person to manage and may require a more experienced, more mature or simply a bigger person. In some cases older people may have problems dealing with more energetic dogs.

13. How much are you willing to spend on your dog's food?
    ☐ Not much – on a tight budget
    ☐ A reasonable amount
    ☐ A good amount
    ☐ No limit

Before getting a dog you should consider how much you are willing to spend on food. It usually costs more to feed larger dogs. If you would like to feed your dog a high-quality food then it may be quite costly to feed a larger dog.

14. How much grooming are you prepared to provide each week?
- ☐ None
- ☐ 1 hour
- ☐ 2½ to 4 hours
- ☐ More than 4 Hours

You should always consider coat type and how much time you are prepared to spend grooming your dog before you get one. Grooming can be time consuming and it can cost you money, whether you groom your dog yourself or hire a professional groomer.

A dog's grooming needs will depend on her coat type. Dogs with short, smooth coats will require the least amount of grooming. Medium long coats will need to be brushed and bathed more often. Long coats will usually require frequent grooming and bathing. Wiry coats may require professional clipping or stripping.

Cost can vary depending on where you live, the quality of the groomer, and how often you need to have your dog groomed. If you are grooming your dog yourself you should plan on bathing your dog, at a minimum, once a month. You should add equipment costs, shampoo and conditioner to your budget, and make allowances for the time you will need to put in, especially when considering whether you want to take care of a dog with extensive grooming needs.

15. Are you looking for a dog that will protect you and your property?
- ☐ No
- ☐ Some warning barks are okay
- ☐ Defensive

You will also need to consider why you want a dog and how much barking you are willing to tolerate. Most dogs will bark to warn of an intruder. However, some dogs are much more prone to barking than others. The little Petit Basset Griffon Vendeen, a wonderful dog, makes a terrible apartment dog because they are so prone to barking. Most hound breeds have a tendency to bark. Other large dogs may also bark a lot as a prelude to defending their home.

16. Do you or your family members suffer from animal/hair allergies?
   ☐ No
   ☐ Yes

If you or your family members suffer from dog allergies then you should make sure that you will be able to tolerate having a dog before getting one. Choose a breed that is known for being more amenable to allergy-sufferers, such as the Bichon Frise, the Portuguese Water Dog, the Maltese, or one of the Poodles (any size). These breeds have single coats and shed less than other breeds.

People with allergies are not actually allergic to dog hair but to the saliva and dander on the hair, but dogs with single coats which shed less tend to have less dander and saliva to spread.

17. Do you have children or child visitors?
   ☐ Yes
   ☐ No

Before getting a dog it is important to consider whether or not you have children. Children and dogs don't always get along well so you need to choose a breed that is known for getting along well with kids. Golden Retrievers and Labradors are two of the best breeds for getting along with kids, followed by Boxers.

Seven Steps to Choosing a Friendly and Compliant Dog

People choose a puppy the same way they choose a car. Some like the color and look and the deal is done. Others inspect it more closely, checking for handling and other characteristics. The good thing about cars is that they don't misbehave! Unfortunately, the same can't be said of dogs. Buying a puppy is an exciting time because you are basically adding a new member to your family, and you want a dog that will be a joy to have and can be easily trained. So, how do you go about finding the right puppy? Well, if you can road test a car, why not road test a puppy?

If you are looking for a dog that will make a great pet and is receptive to proper training, then you should be looking for a puppy that is not too bossy or too timid. The best puppies are those that are curious, friendly yet compliant. Every dog is different and so it can be hard to know what to look for. Here is my seven-step road test you can use when selecting your puppy at a pet store or breeder's premises:

Observe the puppy at play. Bossy puppies generally bite, growl at or pin down other puppies. Compliant puppies tend to play more nicely.

Approach and pat the puppies. The bossy puppy will *demand* your attention and affection, even when you are patting the other puppies. Curious puppies will seek your attention in a friendly way.

Pick up the puppy and cradle it like a baby. Puppies that resist and wriggle are generally more bossy than those that are compliant.

If you can, have the puppies follow you around and see which ones lead the pack and which puppies stay away. The puppies at the front of the pack are either curious or bossy. The bossy ones will tend to fend off other puppies in your presence.

Place an unfamiliar item near the puppies. (Make sure the item is light, quiet and non-threatening). Puppies that investigate immediately or after a couple of moments are more likely to be curious and secure than those that stay away from the object altogether.

Ensure the puppies are in an enclosed space and walk away from the puppies. Observe which puppies settle down quietly and which puppies show insecurity by yapping and whining.

Observe the breeder or pet store attendant with the puppies. The puppies that seemed initially timid to you may turn out to be quite friendly towards someone they know. This means the puppy may need time to warm up to you. This is fine as cautious puppies still make great pets if trained to socialize well.

A puppy that performs well in all (or most) of these tests is likely to make a curious, friendly and compliant companion. To ensure your puppy continues to develop a healthy personality, proper socialization and training is highly recommended.

The Process of Choosing a Puppy from the Pound

Lots of people like the idea of getting a dog from the pound. All over the world millions of dogs pass through animal shelters each year for various reasons. Many people find very good pets at the pound. Of course, if you go to an animal shelter it can be a little overwhelming, especially if there are many dogs. It may be hard to make a choice. It's best to know what you're looking for before you go. If you make an informed decision then you're less likely to have a bad experience with a shelter dog.

Behavioral and health considerations

One of the drawbacks of getting a dog from the pound is the fact that you often have less information about a dog's history. You may see a few dogs that you like but the shelter staff probably won't know much or anything about the dogs' parents or health histories. If a dog has parents with genetic diseases, for example, you won't know it. If an adult dog has early hip dysplasia, there may not be signs of it yet.

However, dogs at the pound are typically examined by staff veterinarians and they are up-to-date on basic vaccinations. They should not be showing any obvious signs of illness, such as having a runny nose or a temperature. It is possible for dogs at the shelter to pick up viruses from each other, such as parvovirus, and to incubate them for a few days. A dog from the pound may seem fine when you take her home but she may become sick a few days later, so if you do get a dog from the pound you need to watch her carefully for several days to make sure that she remains healthy.

Dogs from many pounds may also be spayed or neutered before you get them, or you may get a voucher so you can have one of these procedures done after you take your dog home. This is usually included in the price of adopting the dog.

From a behavioral standpoint, dogs from the pound can be a mixed bag so you will need to choose carefully. These days it's getting harder and harder to find puppies at animal shelters thanks to the large number of owners who spay and neuter their dogs. This means that most of the dogs you see will probably be young adults or older dogs. Many owners turn in young adult dogs when they start to show some rambunctious behavior (too much barking, housebreaking problems, jumping on people, chewing, and so on). This means that the young dogs you see may have some behavioral issues but they are the kind of problems that can be solved if you are willing to work on them. However, they will take patience and training. These dogs may not be a good choice for a first-time dog owner. If you do want to adopt one of these dogs with some basic training problems it's usually a good idea to sign up for training classes as soon as possible.

Some dogs at the pound may have behavioral issues that stem from more complicated problems such as neglect or abuse. Again, these problems can be managed but they usually take a long time and they most often need an experienced dog owner to help them.

Of course, you may find a dog at the pound who just needs a good home and who doesn't have many, if any, behavioral problems. These dogs make a good choice for any owner.

Puppy or adult dog?

Both puppies and adult dogs have their advantages. Everyone loves a cute, adorable puppy. However, they require lots of time. They have to be housetrained and they have to be taught not to chew or destroy things in the house. They have to be taught basic manners. They don't usually know much of anything at the start. Plus, it's often hard to find puppies at animal shelters these days.

Adult dogs are often already housetrained. They often already have some good manners and may know some basic training commands. Adult dogs are usually calmer and cause less mayhem in the home than a puppy does. Even if an adult dog does have one or two quirks, such as needing to learn to stop barking so much, it can be easier to work on one issue instead of trying to teach a puppy everything she needs to learn. Plus, adult dogs may sit in shelters waiting for a home for longer than puppies, which are adopted immediately, so you would be doing a good deed by adopting an older dog. You know what you're getting with an older dog.

What to ask at the pound

When you go to the pound to see the dogs you will likely be shown the dogs available for adoption. Many shelters have an area where you can interact with the available dogs. If you find a dog that you like you should ask what the staff knows about her history: where did she come from? Who turned her in? Why is she there? It's a good idea to try to find out as much as you can about any dog you like. The staff may or may not know much since they get dogs in various ways. Be aware that the shelter staff are not always very good at identifying dogs. They may tell you that a dog is a "Lab-Beagle mix" when, in fact, the dog is a Schipperke or some other kind of dog. Many black dogs are labeled as Labradors or Labrador mixes. Many mixed breed dogs are described as purebred dogs when they aren't. So, be aware of these facts.

The process of adopting

In order to adopt a dog from the pound you should plan to visit and see the dogs. It's best not to make a snap decision, although if you wait it's possible that the dog you like could be gone. Do find out all you can from the staff about the dog that you like. Spend time petting and playing with the dog, if possible. Some private shelters may have you fill out an application and try to check your references, but most public shelters will simply have you fill out a form to get the dog you like. There is always a fee to adopt a dog. This fee can vary widely depending on the pound but it usually includes the dog's vaccinations and it can include the dog's spaying/neutering or a voucher to have this procedure done. You will also need to get the dog's license and registration if these are required where you live.

Demonstrating You Are a Suitable Owner

Some private shelters will have you fill out a form that is similar to an adoption form asking you about your home life, your job, your family, your other pets, what kind of yard and fence you have, and so on. They will check up on you to see if you are a suitable owner. And they may refuse to allow you to adopt a dog. However, most public shelters and pounds will simply allow you pay the fee to adopt a dog, let you get the dog's registration and license and take the dog home.

Costs

United States and Canada

In the US, costs at public pounds for adopting a dog can be anywhere from around USD25 to close to USD150. Most pounds charge around USD75 to adopt a dog. Private shelters may charge much more to adopt a dog.

You can find a list of American and Canadian shelters here.

United Kingdom

If you're interested in adopting a dog in the United Kingdom, then you can check out the The Dog Rescue Pages. When adopting a dog in the United Kingdom, most organizations will ask for a contribution from you of between £70 and £120.

Australia

If you're interested in adopting a dog in Australia, then you can check out the Pet Rescue Directory. Adopting a dog in Australia can cost anywhere between AUD50 and AUD350.

Introducing Puppy to Your Home

A new puppy has many things to learn when you first bring her home. She is coming from living with her mother and siblings. Her mother has likely been taking care of everything and she's used to playing and living in a group. Now that she's left her home and come to live with you, things are going to be very different. She may be an only dog now, or she is with dogs and cats that she doesn't know. Her mother is gone. She doesn't know the place or the rules anymore. It's up to you to introduce her to the household and help her fit in.

You can help your new puppy begin adjusting by showing her around when you first bring her home. This is especially helpful if you have a yard and you want your puppy to start relieving herself in the yard. It may take a while before your puppy is potty trained but if you show her around the yard when she arrives and give her a chance to relieve herself before going indoors, you can get her started on a good note.

It's a good idea to set up boundaries in the house so your puppy will know where she is and is not allowed. This will help your puppy with her house training by limiting her to certain rooms. It will also limit the areas where she can play or potentially tear things up. You should pay particular attention to puppy proofing these rooms. You can purchase baby gates or dog gates and set them up across doorways to keep your puppy from going into certain areas of the house.

If you have other dogs or cats you should plan carefully how you will introduce your puppy to them. You should not simply turn your puppy loose and allow her to get in the face of your current pets. That is a sure way for your puppy to be scratched, bitten or growled at. It will not end well for your puppy. Instead of allowing your puppy to rush up to your older dog or cat, it's a good idea to separate them with the dog gates or to place the puppy in a crate or pet carrier and let your pets get to know each other more slowly. It may take several days before you can completely introduce your puppy to your current pet but if you take your time the introduction will go much better. Do not rush things. Allow the animals to get to know each other. Your current pet may resent the new puppy but, in time, she will probably accept it.

You will need to teach your puppy many basic things such as where to eat and where to sleep, along with her house training lessons. All of these things are quite normal. Your puppy should start learning them very quickly. It may take a few weeks before your puppy is fully house trained but she will learn if you are patient and consistent. Virtually every puppy can be house trained if the owner is persistent.

If you are having problems with your puppy listening to you then you should consider signing up for a puppy preschool or puppy kindergarten class with your puppy. These classes are good ways to socialize your puppy, which is always a good idea; they also provide some basic lessons in good manners. From these classes you can easily move on to some basic obedience classes with your puppy. Every dog needs to know a little basic obedience. The better trained your puppy is, the better she will behave at home, and the happier you will both be.

Checklist: Puppy Care in the First 24 Hours

The day you bring home your new puppy will be one of the most exciting days in your relationship. That first day is the start of your life together; there's so much fun and happiness ahead for you both. To make the first 24 hours smooth for you and your puppy, there are some practical things you should take care of.

Here's a look at what to do with your new puppy in the first 24 hours:

What you should have

It is important to do some planning ahead so you have all the things your puppy will need ready and waiting when she arrives. Your puppy will need:

- A collar and leash.
- Bowls or pans for food and water.
- The same dog food she's been accustomed to eating (you can find this out from the pet store, shelter or breeder).
- A place to sleep such as a dog bed or crate.
- A good brush and comb for grooming.
- Don't forget the toys! It is also a good idea to have some safe things for your puppy to chew on so she won't be tempted to chew on your shoes or the furniture. You will probably also want to get some papers or a house training patch to get your puppy started on potty training.

Taking your puppy home

Whether you're picking your puppy up from a shelter, pet store or breeder, it's usually a good idea to bring your puppy home in a crate in your vehicle. A crate provides some protection for your puppy in case of an accident. They also prevent your puppy from wandering all over the vehicle or interfering with you while you drive, which could cause an accident. A crate usually makes a puppy feel more secure, too. It can also be used later as a place for your puppy to rest and sleep in your home.

What to do as soon as you arrive home

When you arrive home the first thing you should do is take your puppy for a walk in your yard, if possible. Allowing your puppy to explore the yard gives her a chance to relieve herself so she won't have an accident as soon as she enters the house. It also lets her see the yard where you will probably want her to potty. Your yard is also probably more relaxing to your puppy than your house, especially if you have family members waiting to meet your new puppy.

Meeting the family

Once you take your puppy indoors you can let people meet her, but try not to overwhelm your puppy with too much attention all at once. It is a good idea if you limit her to just one or two rooms at first, until she learns the house rules.

Making puppy comfortable

Offer her water; she may be thirsty after her first trip.

Remember to take her outside to potty frequently. If you have put down papers or a house training patch for her, make sure you lead her to the area so she knows where it is.

Keep in mind that your puppy is having a very exciting – and stressful – day. Allow her some time to take a nap if she shows signs of being sleepy. Puppies play hard but they also rest frequently.

Meal and potty times

Your puppy will need to eat multiple times per day, depending on her age. For more information on feeding schedules, see Chapter 2: Nutritious Food for a Well-Fed and Healthy Dog. Be sure to take her outside or to her potty patch/papers right after she eats so she will start getting the hang of house training. For more information on how to potty train your puppy, see Chapter 9: The Sure-Fire Way to Get Your Puppy Potty Trained In a Week.

An appointment with a veterinarian

Before the day is over you should make an appointment for your puppy to get her next set of vaccinations from the veterinarian. It is usually a good idea for a vet to see your new puppy within a day or two of bringing her home in order to make sure that your puppy is healthy and not harboring any diseases, infections or worms.

Bedtime

By bedtime your puppy will probably have stolen your heart completely. You can decide where you want your puppy to sleep. Some people like their puppy to sleep on a dog bed. Others like their puppy to sleep in their crate. And others like to have their puppy sleep on the bed with them. This is a personal decision and it's up to you.

Your puppy may or may not sleep quietly all the way through the night. Some puppies will cry and whimper. If your puppy cries you can give her a toy or stuffed animal and this usually helps to soothe them. Always make sure your puppy doesn't need to go outside to relieve herself. Young puppies may need to go outside at least once during the night because they have a small bladder.

The next morning

Most people are already bonded to a new puppy within the first 24 hours. By the time you wake up the next morning (or your puppy wakes you up!), your puppy will probably be feeling very energetic and ready to play. Be prepared to wake up early and play with your puppy before you do anything else.

Enjoy your puppy

Your first 24 hours with your new puppy is very exciting. The time usually flies by as you get to know each other. Enjoy this time: one day you'll notice your puppy has become a dog and you'll wonder where the time went! For an enjoyable and safe puppyhood, plan ahead and everything should go very smoothly.

The Right Equipment

You can make your first days together go much more smoothly with a little planning, and your new puppy will be much happier as a result.

Here is a brief checklist of the things you will need before you bring your new puppy home:

1. Your puppy will need a flat buckle collar and leash. A nice nylon collar and leash will do very well. There is no need to spend a lot of money on an expensive collar at this stage or to buy something made of leather. Your puppy will be growing quickly and will soon outgrow her first collars. Buy something that is practical and safe. You may wish to get a collar that is brightly colored in case your puppy wanders away from you – something bright will make her easier to spot. Her leash should be about six feet long.
2. Your puppy will need a crate for sleeping and house training. Even if you don't plan to have your puppy sleep in the crate on a regular basis, all dogs should be crate-trained. It is recommended that dogs ride in crates when in vehicles (or use a harness), and most dogs must ride in a crate if they fly by plane. Choose a crate that is large enough for your dog to stand up and turn around in but not so large that she will be tossed around in case of a car accident. Dogs can be injured in crates if the crate is too large.

3. You will also need to choose appropriate grooming equipment for your puppy. You can start with a good boar-bristle brush and a greyhound comb (a long metal comb with one-inch teeth). Long-coated breeds will probably need a pin-brush. Your puppy will also need a good shampoo and conditioner. You should try to choose a shampoo and conditioner that is suited to your puppy's coat. An Afghan Hound will have different shampoo and conditioning needs than an Airedale, for instance. Some coats are naturally silky and soft while others are harsh and wiry. Shampoos and conditioners are usually labeled to state what kind of dogs or coats they are made for. If you have any questions about what kind of grooming supplies you should get, you should ask the advice of your dog's breeder or someone familiar with your kind of dog.

4. Make sure that you have toys for your puppy before you bring her home. Your puppy will be coming into a strange home and she will appreciate something fun to cheer her up. Choose a few things from different toy categories such as balls, ropes, squeakies, stuffed animal-type toys, and so on. Your puppy will soon let you know what kind of toy she likes best.

5. Don't forget basic things like food and water bowls and some food for your puppy. You should try to get the same kind of food that she's been used to eating. Sometimes breeders will send some food home with you so your puppy's diet won't be interrupted. As far as bowls are concerned, metal or ceramic bowls are usually best since they don't trigger allergies in dogs.

6. Finally, make sure that your puppy has a bed. The bed can be a mat, a nice stuffed dog bed or a rug. I highly recommend an enclosed bed, like a crate or kennel, as the dog will be secure and warm in colder times – some dogs will roam around at night due to restlessness brought about by being cold or uncomfortable. This can lead to barking and destruction. Be aware that wherever your puppy starts sleeping in the beginning, she will likely continue to sleep there. So, if you don't want your puppy sleeping on the bed, don't let her get comfortable there!

If you follow these suggestions, and remember to puppy-proof the house by securing things the puppy shouldn't eat or destroy, your puppy's first days in your home should go very well.

Budgeting for Your Puppy's Needs

Dog ownership today can be surprisingly expensive. If you already own a dog then you have probably noticed that dog food prices seem to be constantly rising, vet costs go up, and most other things associated with keeping your dog happy and healthy are costing you more. Of course, the costs of owning a dog have to be considered over your dog's entire lifespan. If you're wondering just how much it costs to keep a dog throughout her life, there has been some research done on the subject.

Based on the 2005-2006 American Pet Product Manufacturers Association (APPMA) National Pet Owners Survey, the average cost per year of owning a dog is around $1571. This means that if your dog lives to be 10 years old, which is not an unreasonable age for most dogs, then you will have spent $15,710 on your dog.

Keep in mind that this is an average figure for all dogs in the United States. Some dogs may live longer or shorter lives. Some owners may spend much more on veterinary costs, especially if their dog has a serious health problem. Costs to keep a dog in an urban area are frequently much higher than in a rural area. If you have to use dog walkers or dog sitters it will add considerably to these costs. Food choices can also add to the costs: for example, if you choose to feed your dog organic or grain-free food you will pay much more than the average dog owner.

On the other hand, there are some costs that all dog owners can expect to have in common:

- Vaccinations.
- Parasite control such as heartworm preventive, treatments for fleas and ticks, worming.
- City, county or state licenses.

- Typical dog supplies such as a collar and leash, water and food bowls, a crate, bedding, toys.
- Dog food and treats.
- Grooming (whether you do it yourself of have it professionally done).
- Cleaning supplies.
- Training classes such as obedience or other classes for your dog.
- Possible boarding if you go on vacation.
- Fencing or other forms of containment for your dog.
- Regular veterinary care beyond vaccinations such as routine examinations, any lab work or x-rays, periodic dental cleaning and treatment for the occasional injury.
- Medications or supplements.

In addition, some owners may choose to purchase pet health insurance, although the number of people using pet health insurance in the U.S. is still very low. You should also factor in pet deposits for your dog if you are renting property or vacationing with your pet. And, some owners may need to buy warm clothing for their dogs.

Taken altogether, these expenses can add up to a tidy sum on an annual basis!

Most people spend the largest amounts on their dog during the first and last years of their dog's life. Puppy vaccinations and supplies can add up during the first year. And, in the later years of your dog's life she may need some extra veterinary support to be comfortable.

When you add these expenses together you will see that any initial sum you pay for your dog is the smallest part of your investment in dog ownership. Whether you get your dog from a breeder or from a shelter (usually for a cost), the real cost of dog ownership comes in the months and years ahead.

Chapter 2
Nutritious Food for a Well-Fed and Healthy Dog

Dogs are amazingly hardy animals. The dog's ancestor – the wolf – was a meat eater but over thousands of years, dogs have adapted to a diet consisting of meat, vegetables and yummy human leftovers! Dog's stomachs are very acidic which can digest bones and fats relatively well. Having said that, a good diet will ensure your dog encounters few health problems, including stomach and intestinal issues.

In this chapter, I'll explain:

- Physical signs your dog is enjoying a healthy diet.
- The right diet and feeding schedules for puppies as they grow.
- The correct amount to feed your dog throughout every stage of life.
- How to prevent food aggression.
- Different diets available for dogs, such as raw, commercial and dry food.
- How to tell the difference between nutritious and dodgy food when reading the labels on packaging.
- How to take care of a dog's dietary requirements during pregnancy and when the dog becomes a senior.
- Tips on overcoming fussy eating habits.
- Which 20 'human' foods and other materials are bad for dogs.
- One smart trick to help with poor digestion.

The Right Diet for Your Puppy

The right diet makes a big difference in your dog's vitality and wellbeing. Here are some signs that your dog is enjoying a healthy diet:

- They poop once to twice daily, their poop being firm, small, brown, relatively of low odor and free of worms (or larvae).
- They have a shiny coat and are energetic.
- They have a reasonable concentration span, which is sufficient for training.
- Their teeth are in good to excellent condition. (Ensure your dog's diet is supplemented by dental chew toys or dental treats.)

There's no one ideal diet for puppies, however feeding your puppy cheap supermarket brands is not recommended. The key is to ensure that your puppy's food intake consists of the correct proportion of protein, calcium and minerals, which will provide steady growth and development.

When choosing the right diet for your puppy, bear in mind that:

1. If you got your puppy from a reputable breeder, then follow the breeder's recommendations. Your breeder should be able to provide good nutritional information.
2. If you are unable to get guidance from the person from whom you obtained your puppy, then purchase high quality puppy food. Do not substitute dog food for puppy food. Dog food does not contain the correct ratio of ingredients for proper development of young dogs.
3. Puppies need a high calcium intake as an insufficient amount can cause bone abnormalities. Having said that, excessive calcium and a diet too high in energy can cause excessive growth spurts and extra weight gain which could damage a puppy's joints.
4. Puppies need protein. Protein is required for growth and nutrition, without which a puppy can develop malformed bones and joints. However, the amount of protein in adult dog food should be 22% or higher than puppy food.

Do not overwhelm your puppy's digestive system by regularly experimenting with new foods or treats.

If you want to feed your puppy a raw or home-cooked diet, consult a vet for guidance. Find an experienced person who has successfully raised puppies to adulthood on your proposed diet. This is critical as raw diets can easily go wrong with puppies – calcium levels should be watched, as well as bacterial contaminants (which can cause grave illnesses).

Make sure your dog has access to fresh water at all times throughout her life. Some owners limit their puppy's access to water at bedtime to discourage night time potty accidents – for more information on this aspect of puppy care see Chapter 9: The Sure-Fire Way to Get Your Puppy Potty Trained In a Week.

Feeding schedules for your puppy

Follow these feeding schedules for puppies at different ages:

- Up to 3 months old: three times a day. (Some vets recommend four times a day for toy breeds).

- Between 2 months and 3 months, you can begin to gradually wean your dog down to two meals a day.
- From three to twelve months old: twice daily. If your dog is fed only once a day, your dog might feel hungry – after all, 24 hours between meals is a long wait!

Amount of food for your puppy

As a starting point go with the amounts recommended by either the packaging, on commercial food, or expert (breeder/vet) suggestions. Adjustments may be needed if you find your puppy becoming overweight (tubby) or underweight (ribby). Making adjustments can be tricky, as puppies experience growth spurts and gangly stages. If unsure, consult your vet. Experts generally agree that your puppy's weight should err on the side of slender, rather than tubby!

Larger breeds grow faster and, as such, more adjustments may need to be made as they transition between the gangly and growth stages at a faster pace.

Puppy treats

Treats should be given only occasionally and are ideally used as rewards during training sessions. Treats should be very small and soft. If you are using commercial treats, then break them down into smaller pieces. Natural alternatives are chopped vegetables (no onion or garlic – they are poisonous to dogs), cooked meat and unsalted popcorn.

Refusing meals

Puppies may refuse a meal if their mouth hurts as a result of teething. If a puppy refuses more than two meals, call your vet.

Preventing Food Aggression in Puppies

Food guarding is a highly undesirable habit. Luckily, it's the easiest problem to prevent. Follow these quick and easy steps at puppy's feeding time:

1. After you set your puppy's food bowl down, start to teach your dog to sit and wait for her food. This way she'll understand that you are the pack leader and have dibs over any food.
2. Once your puppy starts eating, place your fingers in the bowl and allow your puppy to eat around your fingers.
3. Pat your dog whilst she is eating so she becomes accustomed to being touched while eating. Do not pull your dog away or taunt her as she eats, as this will only serve to annoy her and encourage aggressive behavior.

The Right Diet for an Adult Dog

An adult dog is generally over one year old, although smaller dogs reach maturity at about 18 months. At this point, the dog will no longer be growing in height, though she may still be gaining weight. This is caused by the development of muscle tone and a process known as 'filling out' – a process that takes a lot of energy. The dog will require this much energy from her food and only a high quality, active dog food source will provide the nutrients that she needs.

Dogs need proteins, minerals, amino acids and fats as part of a healthy diet. Dogs could technically survive on a vegetarian diet, although many dog nutritionists do not recommend this.

Generally speaking, dog owners can choose from three broad types of dog food: commercial food (kibble and canned), raw food, or a blend of the two.

Do not feed the young adult dog food for senior (or old) dogs. This food does not provide the dog with the nutrients that she needs to develop those strong and lean muscles that her body needs to be healthy.

As always, fresh water should be available at all times.

Commercial dog food and how to read commercial dog food labels

Generally cheap kibble and canned dog food will not provide enough nutrients for your dog. If your dog has a lackluster coat, is overly flatulent, in average condition, or has skin problems, chances are you can point the finger directly at what your dog is eating.

A diet that consists solely, or mainly, of wet (canned) food means your dog may be slightly more prone to cavities and tooth decay. This can result in a dog losing her teeth due to disuse and decay. However, this food is ideal for hiding medication because most dogs will scoff it so fast that they won't notice any pills mixed inside.

Remember that slogans like 'Premium Grade', 'Vet Approved', 'Good For Your Dog' and 'Finest Ingredients' are not specific enough to allow you to make an informed decision. When choosing your dog food, disregard the writing on the packaging in favor of reading the ingredients (which are listed in order of highest to lowest quantity). As a friend of mine once said: 'Don't be slack, read the back!"

When reading dog food labels make sure you are able to see the following types of ingredients:

- Animal protein to be listed more than once in the top five ingredients.
- Meats that are clearly listed by type, for example: rabbit, chicken, beef, lamb, duck and venison.
- Whole grains such as millet, rice and oats.
- Naturally preserved kibble.

When reading dog food labels make sure you avoid dog foods that have the following 'ingredients':

- Cheap canned food that contains 'meat chunks' – these may simply be grain gluten processed to resemble meat.
- 'Animal digest' or 'meat meal' – these labels do not guarantee high grade/quality meat.

- Added colors, flavors or artificial preservatives.
- Grain by-products such as gluten and brewer's rice.
- Food that contains soy which causes allergies in many dogs.
- Products where the first listed ingredient is a corn, wheat, meat-meal or meat by-product.

If you're feeding your dog only canned food and kibble, make sure that most of it is kibble. Canned foods are not designed to provide a dog's complete diet. This is partly because canned food does not offer any health benefits to your dog's teeth; kibble results in less teeth tartar. It will also save you a small fortune!

Daily intake of moist food will mean that dogs require, and therefore drink, less water. If you are changing your dog's diet to include more dry food (e.g. from only moist food to moist food plus kibble), make sure that you have more fresh water out for your dog to drink. You may also need to allow your dog a few more toilet breaks whilst she adjusts to her new and healthier diet.

The raw diet

Raw feeding, also known as 'BARF' (Biologically Appropriate Raw Food), promotes a diet of raw meat, bones and organs (with no grains).

The BARF diet consists of:

- 5-10% organ meats
- 10-15% bones
- 75-85% muscle meats
- Small amounts of vegetables (optional)

A warning about vegetables: do not feed your dog onions or garlic. Although most dogs tolerate small amounts of these vegetables, they can result in your dog's death if she eats too much of them. Unfortunately, or fortunately as it means that no one has force fed dogs on copious amounts of onions and garlic, veterinarians don't know exactly what the lethal dose is although I should imagine that it would differ according to breed, size and age as well as the condition of the dog.

If you feed your dog a raw diet, you have to be aware of possible problems arising from ingesting undigested bone, as well as the bacteria and virus inherent in raw meat. Salmonella and Campylobacter bacteria can be an issue with raw chicken meat, and raw pig meat can contain the virus that causes Aujeszky's disease as well as fluke worms. Both can cause serious illness and even death in canines if left untreated. Members of the dog family tend to eat the organs of freshly caught prey and then bury the remains for days or even weeks before eating it. This allows the meat to start to decay in a more hygienic environment than being left in the open air to rot, which results in a degree of digestion of the raw meat. Of course the additional benefit of burying the meat is that it is far less likely to be stolen by other scavengers.

If you do feed raw foods to your dog, make sure that they are very fresh and haven't been on a supermarket shelf for days. The fresher the food, the smaller the chance of contamination with germs and bacteria. Even if you don't ordinarily feed your dog raw food, I would advise you to refrain from giving your dog meat, cooked or otherwise, that has been in the fridge past its Use By or Best Before date, or even in the freezer past the freezer's maximum recommended storage period.

Raw diet principles have now been adopted by dog food companies that produce pre-ground raw dog food. This is particularly useful for owners worried that raw bones may remain undigested in their dog's gut. Alternatively, dog owners may elect to grind bones (using relatively inexpensive home grinders).

How much should you feed your dog?

Dogs are meant to know when they've eaten enough (but then so are we!), however they are usually guided by what their owners feed them. It is not uncommon for dogs to eat then walk away from the bowl with food left in it. They might go and run round for a while or sleep and then return to the bowl only to drink the water and will ignore the food still there until later in the day. Obviously, I would only recommend that you allow this with kibble and not with moist/wet foods as the influx of flies alone would be off-putting! Be aware that the feeding recommendations on commercial dog food will always give you higher end of the requirement range. So if your dog tends to become overweight, reduce the amount you feed her gradually, in order to allow your dog's stomach to tighten. Remember how you feel when you go on a diet!

Dogs of different breeds and sizes still have the same digestive system, which means if you own more than one dog you can feed them the same things, but in different quantities. If you have multiple dogs, there may be a temptation to save on dog food expenses by purchasing a cheaper brand – but you should avoid this temptation. It can take several times the amount of cheap dog food to provide the same nutritional value offered by higher quality food. Owners often think they are saving money this way when, in fact, it is the other way around. However, you do not always get what you pay for – which is why, again, you must read and understand the ingredients label and the recommended quantities. Some inexpensive dog foods may be nearly as good, if not as good, as some of the more expensive brands.

I would recommend you visit your local supermarket and local pet food shop, and even a farm supplies shop, with a pen and a pad and write down and compare all of brands. You may find that you can feed your dog just as well with a little less food (fewer poops) and for a little less money. If you do change brands, spend a week or two mixing both the old and new brands, slowly reducing the old food and increasing the new.

The total daily quantities recommended in the system below assume you will be feeding your dog high quality, nutritionally rich food.

Dog Size	Raw Diet*	Dry Food	Dry & Wet Food
Toy 2-4.5kgs (5-10lbs) Toy Poodle Pomeranian Shih Tzu Chihuahua	40-90g (1.4-3.15oz)	70-230g (2.5–8oz)	up to 55g (2oz) & ¼ can
Small 4.5-9kgs (10-20lbs) Dachshund Scottish Terrier	90–180g (1.4-6.3oz)	230-510 g (8-18oz)	115-285g (4-10oz) & ½ can
Medium 9-23kgs (20-50lbs) Beagle Spaniel Bull Dog Poodle	180–460g (6.3-16oz)	510-850 g (18-30oz)	225-560g (8-20oz) & 1 can
Large 23-35kgs (50-77lbs) Labrador Collie Setter Alsatian	460g–1.2kg (16-42oz)	850-1135 g (30-40oz)	395-680 g (14-24oz) & 1 ½ cans
Maxi 35+kgs (77+lbs) Great Dane St Bernard	1.2kg+ (42oz+)	1135g+ (40oz+)	680-1190g (24-42oz) & 2 cans

*In a raw diet, a dog should eat approximately 2% of its ideal body weight per day.

Please note: This chart is an approximation only – the quantity needed also depends on a dog's metabolism and activity level. A good test to see whether your dog is eating enough is to feel her ribs – any dog within the ideal weight range will have a small amount of fat and muscle covering the ribs.

Types of treats

There are some great treats that you can use to train your dog or offer as a snack:

- A great tasty treat, high in protein and used by good dog owners to reward their dogs for obedience, is freeze-dried beef liver. You can also try freeze-dried chicken.
- Many dogs absolutely love bully sticks (they're made of dried bull penis). They're softer than rawhide, and so easy to digest. They will also keep your dog occupied for a long time as they are quite chewy. I recommend giving your dog a bully stick before leaving the dog alone at home, so she has something to occupy herself.
- Although dogs love rawhide and pigs ears, these can shatter or break apart leaving the sharp pieces to wreak havoc on your dog's digestive tract. Make sure the rawhide is compressed. Also, watch for cheap rawhide imitations that are too salty and contain lots of chemicals.
- Brussels sprout stalks are good for your dog. They're also tasty and tough and can be used in fetch games.
- Sugar cane is a great way to reward your dog every once in a while.
- Beef bones from the hip or knuckle of a cow, with the marrow providing a tasty surprise. Brisket bones are good too, and can be eaten quicker than the beef bones. Ensure you don't give your dog too many bones as they can cause constipation. Never give your dog cooked chop or chicken bones as they splinter and can puncture their digestive tracts.

How many treats should be in my dog's diet?

If providing treats or snacks, reduce the volume of your dog's main meals accordingly. Treats should never constitute more than 15% of your dog's overall diet.

Food Throughout a Dog's Life

The later years

Dogs are considered 'seniors' when they have lived to about two-thirds of their expected life span. A large breed dog, such as the Great Dane with a life expectancy of around nine years, may be considered senior at six. Meanwhile, a small breed with a life expectancy of 13 years will be a senior at about nine years.

This does not mean that every 'senior' dog behaves like a senior dog and should be fed and handled like a senior. Just as there are many senior people who still lead very active lives, there are senior dogs that are more active than others.

Two particular health issues may arise as your dog ages:

1. Weight gain – older dogs are prone to gaining too much weight, as they often exercise less and eat more. Obesity can then lead to serious health problems such as diabetes, kidney failure, heart disease and dental problems.
2. Arthritis – most dogs will suffer some degree of arthritis from a certain age onwards. The more overweight a dog is, the more pain she will experience from her arthritis.

Most senior or mature dog foods are low-calorie foods. The food will still offer the right balance between fats, calories and carbohydrates, and there is an increase in fiber. Wheat bran can be added to further increase the fiber in the dog's food, helping prevent constipation. Most senior dog foods are high in fillers because the senior dog is not as active as a young adult dog but is used to eating a specific amount of food and wants to continue to eat this amount of food.

Supplements may be necessary at this stage of your dog's life for her comfort and health. Supplements that help to support joint health can greatly reduce the pain and inflammation caused by arthritis.

Some dogs have trouble with solid kibble pieces as they begin to age, because of the poor condition of their teeth. If this is the case, then your dog may need to be kept off solid dry dog food and introduced to canned or homemade dog food.

Make the change gradually to prevent gastrointestinal indigestion. You could also add a small amount of wet food to the dog food or add water or broth to the food to soften it.

On top of that, get your vet to check the teeth regularly in case they need cleaning. Older pets benefit from more frequent examinations and regular blood tests. This way any potential problems can be caught in the early stages, and a lot of pain and discomfort can be prevented this way.

Sporting breeds

Sporting dogs are dogs bred for hunting small game. These are naturally very active dogs. These dogs can be of any breed or mix breed and vary in size.

Most people think of the hunting dog when they think of sporting dogs. However, there are many sports that dogs can participate in. The fastest growing sports for dogs include Agility and Fly Ball. Both of these sports are fast paced and require a lot of energy and concentration from your dog. Other sports can include sledding and weight pulling. These are endurance and strength sports that demand even more from the dog's physique.

Food that is geared especially to the sporting dog is higher in protein and fat than the average dog food. The increase in protein helps the dog to keep muscles strong and ligaments supple. This also helps to make the dog feel full for a longer time, helping her perform better during the competitions or throughout a highly energetic day.

A high fat content helps replace calories that the dog burns during her activities. These calories help to give the dog the energy she needs to be active longer.

Sporting dog foods might also contain supplements that will support the high nutritional needs of the active dog. These might include probiotics to assist the dog's digestion. The most common of these probiotics is FOS (fructooligosaccharides). Glucosamine and chondroitin sulfate are joint supplements that are often added into sporting dog foods to assist in the protection and lubrication of the joints.

Fish oil is often added to the food as well to help support the heart and the skin of the dog. Anti-oxidants are added to help eliminate the free-radicals that intense exercise causes. These free radicals can hinder your dog's performance and can even cause serious conditions such as cancer in the long term.

Your sporting dog will also require a lot of water. Water is essential to her bodily functions and will help her to remain active. Make sure water is always available, especially at the sporting events that she will be attending.

Feeding a pregnant bitch

Just like a pregnant women, a pregnant bitch needs special food and care. Specific nutrients and calories will guarantee that the pups develop correctly, and will also ensure her health and well-being through pregnancy, birth and lactation periods.

Pregnancies last around 63 days in dogs – that's about 9 weeks in total.

During the first 5 weeks of the pregnancy, all you need to do is make sure that the bitch gets enough water. At this stage, the puppies are not growing much and aren't very taxing for her body. However, she will experience an increase in blood volume during this time as the fluid-filled sacs that hold the puppies are developed.

Around the third week after mating, a lot of bitches go without food for 7-10 days. During this period they might experience some nausea, just like a woman might. Vomiting during pregnancy is very uncommon in dogs though.

During the first part of the pregnancy, do not give your dog any medications that have not been suggested and approved by your veterinarian. Do not add any supplements to her food, unless instructed to do so by your veterinarian, because the puppies are very vulnerable at this stage of their development.

Bitches do not usually show any discharge from the vagina during pregnancy. If you notice any discharge, especially if it's yellow or green in color or has a strong smell, consult your veterinarian immediately. The dog might have lost the pups and developed an infection.

During the last 4 weeks of the pregnancy, the puppies will begin to grow rapidly. At this stage, you will need to increase the mother dog's food intake by around 25% every week. This means that by the eighth week, you must double the amount of food that you were originally feeding them.

In week six or seven, it is a good idea to start splitting the meals into two portions if you are not already doing so, and in the last week into 3 portions. Her belly will feel very big by then and she simply won't have the stomach to take in a whole meal at a time.

Afterwards, try to gradually increase the amount of food you are giving her to prevent her from stopping eating or getting indigestion.

Nursing

Once the puppies are born, the bitch will still need a large amount of high quality food. At this time, her puppies will be feeding on her milk. It is called the lactation period. It is a common mistake to reduce the amount of food to the bitch while she is nursing, but producing the milk takes a lot of energy. The mother's food intake will drastically affect the amount of nutrients that the puppies get, and insufficient nutrients can have devastating effects on the health of both the bitch and the puppies.

A nursing bitch requires special food and care. She will need food that has a very high amount of protein and calories. Remember that now she is feeding herself and her puppies.

The milk that she is producing contains a lot of calcium. The calcium in the milk comes directly from the blood stream and the bones of the mother. Sudden depletion of calcium can lead to a serious condition called 'eclampsia' or milk fever.

Symptoms to watch out for are panting, lethargy and sudden disinterest in her puppies. Her muscles might start to twitch and she might develop serious cramps all over her body and have a fever. This is an emergency situation and you must take her straight to the vet. The vet will administer calcium (usually through an intravenous drip) and this usually leads to fast recovery.

If in any doubt about your canine mom's nutritional needs, talk to your veterinarian. He or she will also help you decide if your bitch needs extra calcium or other minerals.

A nursing dog will also need a lot of water because milk production takes a lot of fluid from her body. Water should be available at all times. Elevating the water bowl can prevent the puppies from spilling the water or falling in and drowning.

At the end of the nursing period, your dog should ideally weigh what she did before the pregnancy. If her weight has decreased, take extra care to bring her back up to her usual condition as soon as the pups have been weaned.

A decrease in weight can affect her during her next pregnancy and for some time after the pregnancy and whelping process.

Is Your Dog the Right Weight?

Checking your dog's weight is important to ensure your dog is within the healthy weight range. You don't need to use a scale and weight chart to find out if your dog has a healthy weight. All you need to do is answer these three simple questions:

1. Can you see the ribs? If you can see the ribs easily, your dog is at least a little underweight. But if they are only slightly visible, then your dog is within the healthy range. If you view your dog from above, you should notice your dog's tapered waist line.
2. Can you feel the ribs? If you can feel the ribs easily as you are stroking her across the ribcage, your dog is of the right weight, with a thin fat cover. If you are having difficulty feeling the ribs under moderate or thick fat cover, then your dog is at least a little overweight.
3. Has your dog got an hourglass shape when viewed from above? If your dog's body goes in radically behind the ribcage, this indicates that she is underweight. However, if your dog's waist tapers in slightly, then she is within the normal weight range. If your dog's back is broader at the waist, she is overweight.

Top View of Dogs at Various Weights

Slim dog

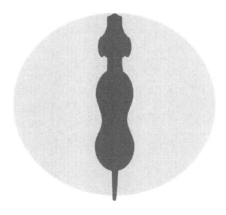

Slightly overweight dog

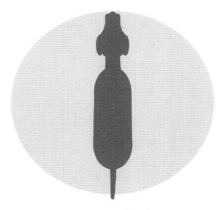

Overweight dog

Other signs your dog is not within a healthy weight range

If your dog is the right weight, she will be reasonably active and energetic. If your dog is lazy, easily worn-out and hesitant to go for walks, she could be either overweight or underweight.

If you believe your dog is overweight or underweight, consult your veterinarian to confirm or allay your suspicions. If your vet recognizes that your dog needs help with her weight, then you can discuss how to improve your dog's health with diet and/or exercise.

Your dog is considered obese if she weighs 15% more than the standard accepted weight for the dog's height.

Varying Your Dog's Diet

After reading this guide you may want to change your dog's diet. People often debate whether a dog can get bored with her diet. Although dogs do enjoy variety in their diet, dogs are capable of thriving on the same diet for long periods, as long as the diet is nutritious and balanced. Therefore, you can choose to stick with a certain diet or you can change it to provide your dog with some variety. Dogs can be very sensitive to regular dietary changes, so don't disrupt their diets too often.

How to change your dog's diet

When changing your dog's diet, do it gradually. Initially your dog's meal should mainly consist of the 'old' food, with a small amount of the 'new' diet. Slowly increase the amount of new food whilst simultaneously decreasing the amount of the old diet. Eventually, the new diet will be 100% of your dog's meal. Alternatively, you can have the same diet and add some supplements to give your dog some variety.

Four Tips for a Fussy Eater

Often dogs can get quite picky about their food, some dogs will test you out by refusing to eat until they get what they really want.

Consult a veterinarian if you are concerned that your dog is being overly fussy, as there might be an underlying health issue. Once illness or disease is ruled out as a possible cause, then try any of these four tips:

1. Apple cider vinegar – a small amount a day mixed in with some moist food will encourage your dog to eat. A teaspoon a day should be enough for 40 pound (18 kilogram) dogs, or a little less for smaller dogs.
2. Crush freeze-dried beef liver and sprinkle over your dog's food. This is also a good source of protein.
3. Leave your dog's bowl out for ten minutes at feeding time. After ten minutes, remove the bowl even if your dog did not eat. Then do the same at the next scheduled feeding time. Do not allow

your dog to have access to any food in between mealtimes. Most dogs will quickly get the message and eat their food within the ten minute time limit lest they miss out! This may seem like a heart-wrenching thing to do for any loving dog owner, but dogs are amazingly adaptable and – if there are no pre-existing health issues – will not suffer from having missed just one meal. (In my experience, that's all it takes!)

4. Instead of feeding your dog from a bowl, use their meal as training treats. All you need to do is separate their meal into smaller portions and give each portion as a reward for obedience. Your dog will come to associate reward with food as well and you are giving her a reason to eat.

Feeding a Pack

When feeding two or more dogs, it is important to make sure every dog gets their own share of food. This can be a little challenging because dogs operate in a hierarchy, which means that dogs higher in the pack may get first dibs at any common food on offer at the expense of lower pack order dogs.

There are a number of things you can do to avoid dogs missing out on their share:

- Each dog should have her own separate bowl and separate feeding area (you might need to ensure each dog cannot get access to another's bowl).
- Supervise feeding time so you can make sure that there is no food stealing.
- Teach all your dogs to sit and wait for their food.
- Ensure you feed each dog the correct amount of high quality, nutritious food.
- Give all your dogs enough time to eat their food: 10 minutes should be enough.

- Have numerous bowls of fresh water available in different spots. (Buckets are ideal as they are hard to tip over when you have dogs jostling nearby.) Big tubs can get dirty as dogs tend to bathe in them.

Digestive Aids

If your dog has stomach problems, diarrhea or is taking antibiotics, then the good bacteria known as Lactobacillus acidophilus dies out, meaning your dog's digestion will not be as effective as it could be.

Yoghurt is a great source of Lactobacillus acidophilus – try giving your dog a teaspoon at mealtimes to help those bacteria grow and thrive.

Remember, that many dogs who are lactose intolerant will suffer from diarrhea if they eat yoghurt. The good news is that you can ask your vet for Lactobacillus acidophilus supplements.

Why dogs eat grass

Dogs get only a nominal amount of nutritional value from eating grass because their digestive system is not equipped to cope with it. The most likely reason a dog eats grass is because it encourages them to vomit, which can be useful when the dog has undigested fur or bone in her stomach.

Hot Spots

Beware of 'hot spots' on your dog's body. These might be caused by an allergic reaction to dog food. Hot spots refer to a warm spot on the body accompanied by hair loss in the same region. The skin may also take on a different color or texture in that region. This is most often caused by an allergy to the carbohydrate and/or animal proteins in a dog's food. Some dogs cannot tolerate grains and will exhibit this allergy as hot spots. If the dog presents these symptoms, consider changing brands of dog food from one that offers grain to one that does not. These alternative foods use potatoes as their form of starch and carbohydrates. These ingredients are not considered potentially dangerous to your dog and they have not been shown to produce hot spots in dogs. The most common potatoes to use are the sweet potato and the red potato.

Poisonous Foods – 20 Things Your Dog Should Never Eat

Here is a list of 20 foods you should never feed your dog. This list is by no means exhaustive, but it covers the most common undesirable 'foods' available:

1. Grapes can cause kidney failure in dogs and can be fatal.
2. Raisins like grapes can cause kidney failure in dogs and can be fatal.
3. Onions contain thiosulphate which is toxic to dogs. They can cause dogs to develop hemolytic anemia (where the red blood cells burst while circulating in the body). Any and all forms of onion can pose a problem, including dehydrated onions, raw onions, cooked onions and table scraps containing cooked onions and/or garlic. Left over pizza, Chinese dishes and commercial

baby food containing onion, sometimes fed as a supplement to young pups, can also cause illness.

Initially, dogs affected by onion poisoning show gastroenteritis with vomiting and diarrhea. They will be disinterested in food and will be dull and weak. The red pigment from the burst blood cells appears in an affected dog's urine and the dog becomes breathless. The breathlessness occurs because the red blood cells that carry oxygen through the body are reduced in number.

The poisoning occurs a few days after the pet has eaten the onion. Onion poisoning can occur with a single ingestion of large quantities or with repeated meals containing small amounts of onion. A single meal of 600 to 800 grams of raw onion can be dangerous whereas a ten-kilogram dog, fed 150 grams of onion for several days, is also likely to develop anemia. The condition improves once the dog is prevented from eating any further onion.

4. Garlic is toxic to dogs for the same reason as onions, however garlic is less toxic and large amounts would need to be eaten to cause illness.

5. Chocolate contains theobromine, which is naturally found in cocoa beans. Although it is not harmful to humans, this substance is highly toxic to dogs (and other domestic animals, such as horses). Theobromine is a stimulant (similar to caffeine) and so affects the central nervous system and heart.

    For instructions on how to handle a situation where a dog has eaten chocolate see Chapter 10: How You Can Avoid Nasty Hazards to Keep Your Puppy Safe and Apply First Aid in Emergencies.

6. Caffeine Products (coffee, coffee grounds, tea and tea bags): drinks and foods containing caffeine cause many of the same symptoms as chocolate.

7. Macadamia nuts and walnuts: Macadamia nuts can cause weakness, muscle tremor and paralysis. You should limit all other nuts as they are not good for dogs in general; their high phosphorous content may lead to bladder stones. An exception

to this rule is peanut butter which can be an effective treat, especially if hidden inside a dog's toy that is designed to hold food, such as a Kong. However, always use salt and sugar free organic peanut butter.

8. Animal fat and fried foods: excessive fat can cause pancreatitis.
9. Cooked bones can splinter and damage a dog's internal organs. A dog chewing on a raw bone should always be supervised as a piece can always break off and cause problems. Try frozen oxtails or frozen knuckle bones then take the bone away before the dog can swallow a final small piece whole. Bones are a great, natural way to clean teeth.
10. Tomatoes can cause tremors and heart arrhythmias. Tomato plants are very toxic to dogs, and tomatoes themselves are unsafe.
11. Avocados: The fruit, pit and plant are all toxic to dogs. They can cause difficulty breathing and fluid accumulation in the chest, abdomen and heart.
12. Nutmeg can cause tremors, seizures and death.
13. The seeds or pits of apples, cherries, peaches, mangos and similar fruit contain cyanide, which is poisonous to dogs as well as humans. Unlike humans, dogs do not know to stop eating at the core/pit and easily ingest them. However, these fruits are generally good for your dog, so remove the pit/seeds before feeding them to your dog.
14. Raw eggs can cause salmonella poisoning in dogs. Dogs have a shorter digestive tract than humans and are not as likely to suffer from food poisoning, but it is still possible. Try organic or scrambled eggs (with no salt).
15. Excessive salt intake can cause kidney problems.
16. Some types of mushrooms can be fatal, so never let your pets chew on mushrooms found in your yard. Safe mushrooms are shiitake, maitake and reishi.
17. Xylitol (a sweetener used in breath mints, gum, mouthwashes and toothpastes). Even a small amount can cause liver failure and death. This is why it is important not to use human toothpaste when brushing your dog's teeth.

18. Sugar and corn syrups: honey and molasses are acceptable in small amounts but should never be given to dogs prone to cancer.

19. Human medications: medicating your dog using medicines designed for people may have serious health implications for your pet. Always seek veterinary advice on what medications to give your dog.

20. Raw potato, skins and potato plants: potato poisonings among people and dogs have occurred. Solanum alkaloids can be found in green sprouts and green potato skins, which occur when the tubers are exposed to sunlight during growth or after harvest. The relatively rare occurrence of actual poisoning is due to several factors: solanine is poorly absorbed; it is mostly hydrolyzed into less toxic solanidinel; and the metabolites are quickly eliminated. Note that cooked, mashed potatoes are fine for dogs, and are actually quite nutritious and digestible.

Chapter 3
The Best Ways to Look After Your Precious Puppy's Coat, Eyes, Ears, Teeth and Paws

Grooming is an essential part of canine care. You should follow a regular and gentle grooming regime from puppyhood. This is because your dog will learn to love the care and attention you provide without resistance and fuss. Plus your dog will reap the benefits of living without the pain or stress associated with bad hygiene and being in a poor condition.

In this chapter, I'll explain:

- How to prevent ear infections by keeping your dog's ears clean and dry.
- When and how to clip your dog's nails safely, without wrestling with your dog.
- Simple ways to keep your dog's teeth clean and her breath fresh.
- How to keep your dog's eyes clean and what to do about common eye, lash and lid complaints.
- How to care for different types of coats and which brushes and combs are suitable.
- The safe and hassle-free way to bathe your dog.

Caring for Your Dog's Ears

Your role as a dog owner is to ensure your dog's ears are kept clean and dry. This will prevent infections, which are not only very painful but can also lead to other complications such as scarring and deafness.

Dogs are particularly susceptible to ear infections if their ears are long-haired and floppy. This is because the hair limits air flow which then allows bacteria to build up around any trapped moisture and debris (like grass seeds, for example).

Regardless of your dog's ear type, here is a list of things you can do to look after your dog's ears:

- Check your dog's ears once a week. If you notice a strong, pungent odor or discharge; reddened ears; or reluctance by your dog to having her ears handled, then take her to the vet. You might also notice your dog shaking her head or scratching her ears more often.
- A small amount of brown wax or dirt in the folds of the outer ear is typical and can be cleaned by wrapping cotton, gauze or a soft cloth around your finger and gently wiping the area.
- Clean your dog's ears once every fortnight.
- Trim the hair from the underside of your dog's ear. You can do this yourself or you can ask your groomer to do so. This increases air flow and prevents the hair from trapping debris which can then make its way to the ear canal.

How to effectively clean your dog's ears

Here are seven steps to cleaning your dog's ears:

1. Take your dog outside to do this as this procedure can be quite messy if your dog shakes her head!
2. Have on hand a veterinary ear wash or 50/50 mixture of tepid water and white vinegar. (Do not use apple cider vinegar.) Double check that the water's temperature is actually tepid (between 20 and 30°C which is between 68 and 86°F).
3. Lay your dog to one side and pull your dog's ear up and out.
4. Gently douche the ear cleaner into the dog's ear. Do not poke or squirt anything into her ears as this can perforate her ear drums.
5. Massage the base of the ear until you hear a squishy sound. Allow your dog to get up and shake – you may find that gunk will be released from her ears (which is why this should be done outside).
6. Clean any gunk off the outer ear by gently wiping it with gauze, cotton or cloth.
7. Repeat the process on the other ear.

Nail Care

Most dogs are reluctant for their paws to be handled and so nail clipping can be quite a tiring activity for many owners. There are four things you can do to ensure that nail clipping does not become an upsetting and frustrating experience for you and your dog:

As soon as you bring your puppy home, start the daily ritual of handling all four of her paws. Pat and lightly squeeze her paws and give her treats and praise; your puppy will learn that having her paws handled by you is nothing to worry about. I'd also recommend using a pair of 'dummy clippers' (clippers with the blades removed) and pretend to clip your puppy's nails often. Whilst dummy clipping, treat and praise your puppy. This way, your puppy won't know the difference between the dummy and the real thing! (Just make sure your dummy and real clippers look similar.)

Ensure your dog has the opportunity to play and exercise on hard surfaces often. This has the effect of naturally wearing your dog's nails, thus reducing the frequency of clipping required.

Take the time to learn how to properly cut your dog's nails. By doing so, you lessen the risk of injuring your dog. The main injury caused by nail clipping is when owners and groomers unintentionally cut the quick of the dog's nail (this causes bleeding and is quite painful). Later, I explain how to cut your dog's nails in the best possible way.

If you are too scared to do it yourself, then take your dog to a reputable groomer or vet. This option is obviously more expensive than DIY, but is worth your peace of mind. Having said that, I have been to a groomer who cut my dog's nails and caused bleeding, so make sure your groomer is experienced and properly trained.

Trimming your dog's nails

No part of the dog's nail should touch and scrape the ground as she walks. If you hear your dog's nails clicking on the floor, then it's time for a trim.

If you don't cut your dog's nails, you run the risk of your dog developing split nails. Split nails are common in dogs and can be quite a nuisance. The split nails will frequently catch on the carpet, blankets and bedding and this can cause some pain. Splitting nails are not usually an indicator of malnutrition or disease but a product of the nails being overly long and not properly trimmed. Regular walks and regular trimming of nails is the best prevention against split nails. Nail files like the 'Peticure' are excellent ways to prevent nail splitting.

Equipment

There are three main types of clippers:

1. Scissor-type clippers. These are ideal for big dog nails. Make sure they're sharp and properly aligned so they don't mash the end of your dog's nails.

2. Guillotine clippers. These are the easiest to use.
3. Battery operated grinders. These take longer but reduce the risk of cutting the quick (although it's not failsafe).

Avoiding the quick

The dog's nail quick contains the blood supply and is the bony base of the nail. The aim of trimming your dog's nail is to cut as close as possible to the quick, without cutting into the quick itself. Dogs with white or light-colored claws have quicks that are visible – the quick is pinkish in color.

It's virtually impossible to see the quick on black nails. Therefore make small nips and start at the tips of the nail. When a small grey area shows in the center of the nail, then you are approaching the quick – it's best to stop at this point.

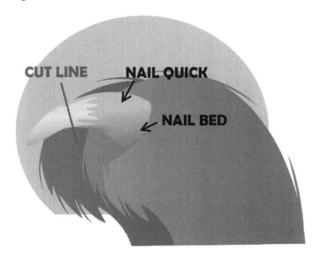

How to trim your dog's nails

Here are some steps to successfully trimming your dog's nails:

1. Ensure that you are relaxed and not in any rush. Have someone assist you.
2. Ensure that you have read the instructions for the clippers and that they are in perfect working order.

3. Choose an enclosed space, so your puppy does not run away if she breaks free.

4. Hold your dog in a hug with your less dominant arm, with the inner forearm resting against your dog's chest. You can then use that hand to hold your dog's paw. Use your other free (dominant) hand to hold the clippers. It's best that your dog is resting in a down position or, for larger dogs, on their side.

5. If your dog fusses or wiggles, don't stop. If you let go, your dog will quickly learn to fuss whenever she does not want you to do something.

6. Align the clipper on the claw, and notice the quick.

7. Cut below the quick to avoid injury and at an angle so the trimmed nail is about parallel to the floor.

8. Trim the nails straight across, being sure that you haven't left any jagged ends that may catch on carpeting or fabric as the animal makes her or her way throughout the house. Don't forget to reward your pet after you are finished and praise her for staying so good.

9. If you strike the quick, it is going to hurt and your dog will bleed. Use light pressure towards the nail to prevent the blood flow. However, this may be challenging as your dog may then squirm, squeal and struggle. The bleeding should not last more than five minutes and you can use styptic powder to stop the flow more quickly.

Dental Care

Dental care is essential for dogs.

Although larger dogs tend to be less susceptible to dental problems than smaller ones, there are exceptions (such as greyhounds) and, like humans, some dogs are simply more prone to these issues.

A dog's healthy teeth are white and healthy gums are pink, with no redness or swelling along the gum line.

Signs of bad dental hygiene include yellowish discoloration, brown residue at the base of the teeth, redness, swelling, bleeding or bad breath. Bad breath can also be a sign of some other underlying medical condition.

If you notice discoloration on one side of the mouth and not the other, then your dog may be chewing on one side to avoid pain. This may be the result of a cracked tooth or other dental issues.

Some people think that it's normal for all dogs to have bad breath, but this is not the case. If your dog's breath smells, then your dog might be experiencing gum disease and bad teeth. The odor is caused by bacteria and infection which, if left untreated, can cause serious dental problems and can be quite painful for your dog.

Your dog may not show signs of discomfort or soreness as dogs often adapt to their lot in life. So, if you notice bad breath but no other symptoms, don't be shy about approaching your vet. Some dogs may refuse their food (as chewing causes further pain).

Dogs need good dental hygiene routine as much as people do. They don't usually get cavities but they are prone to plaque and tartar (which is the ugly brown buildup you see on some dogs' teeth). Plaque and tartar can lead to bad breath and more serious dental problems. You can keep your dog's teeth pearly white and remove plaque by regularly brushing her teeth.

Brushing is essential to keeping your dog's teeth clean and removing the slight yellowing caused by tartar. Brushing is recommended daily or at least several times a week. There are brushes made for dogs that are angled to fit into your dog's mouth. Some people prefer to use small dental pads or rubber "fingers" that fit over their finger. They can then slip this little rubber piece into their dog's mouth to do the brushing.

There are also toothpastes that are specially made for dogs. These toothpastes come in flavors that are designed to appeal to a dog's taste buds such as peanut butter, beef and so on. Most dogs consider these pastes to be treats so after you introduce them to your dog it's easy to get your dog to open up and let you brush her teeth.

Be warned: human toothpaste is fatal to dogs. Never use human toothpaste when brushing your dog's teeth.

Brushing your dog's teeth is very much like brushing your own teeth. The only real difference is that you will need to make sure you brush far in the back of your dog's mouth since dogs have such long, deep jaws. Make sure you concentrate on the outside of the dog's teeth since many dogs get tartar buildup in this area.

Even with good brushing your dog will probably need to have her teeth professionally cleaned by your veterinarian occasionally. Vets can also talk to you about appropriate mouth washes and toothpaste with special enzymes that help dissolve tarter.

In addition to brushing, there are various other foods or treats that will help keep your dog's teeth and gums clean:

- Raw meaty bones.
- Marrow bones.
- Frozen poultry.
- Kong toys.
- Giant Nylabones.
- Nylon bones (some are flavored but you can also soak them overnight in meat broth to add flavor).
- Greenies.
- Bully sticks.
- Dentastix.
- High quality grain-free kibble.

Be careful of giving your dog large bones from the butcher; aggressive chewers may crack their teeth on these.

Fresh breath

If your dog's breath is stinky and your vet has given your dog's teeth the all clear, then your dog may be eating some smelly items. Perhaps she found something foul in the yard such as an animal carcass or garbage. Maybe she's a dog who eats poop? You can try to get her to stop paying attention to these things but, in the meantime, it will also help if you give her some better-tasting things on which to chew. Try some good oral chews recommended by the Veterinary Oral Health Council, such as Canine Greenies or a good mint-flavored chew to freshen her breath.

You can also give your dog treats for good breath. There are a number of dog treats that claim to improve a dog's breath. Some of them are mint-flavored or have other flavors that are more appealing to dogs, such as beef. Try some and see if your dog likes them.

Eye Care

If your puppy's eyes are healthy, then all you need to do is simply wipe some gunk from your dog's eyes with a damp cloth occasionally. There are also various brands of eyewash that can be used to flush out debris, dust or other irritants from your dog's eyes. One such product is called Eye Clens. You can also use eye washes with herbal formulas that have anti-bacterial properties; these include chamomile, calendula and goldenseal.

Tear stains

The most common eye issue in dogs is tear stains. Tear stains are especially common among breeds with light or white-colored fur such as the Cocker Spaniel, Poodle and Shih Tzu. The rusty-colored discharge can be rather unsightly and can emit a strong odor.

Causes of Tear Stains

There are many causes of tear stains, ranging from allergies, diet, poor health, infection and genetic predisposition. Infected tear ducts are a common cause of excess moisture, which will result in staining.

Tear stains can be a sign of a foreign body in the eye, injury, allergies or conjunctivitis. Conjunctivitis usually results in a greenish stain. Genetics, affecting eye structure, may result in excess tears.

Apart from staining, other symptoms of poor health that manifest in dogs' eyes can be cloudiness, inflammation or bleeding. If these symptoms appear, seek immediate veterinary attention.

Staining can also be caused by your dog consuming water with excess minerals.

Cleaning Stains

If your dog is otherwise healthy, then staining can be managed by cleaning the area under your dog's eyes. A very important part of puppy and dog care is cleaning stains regularly, as the dampness can be a breeding ground for bacteria and yeast. Cleaning should be done with care since dogs' eyes are just as sensitive as those of humans.

Here are some options for cleaning stains:

- Mix equal parts corn starch and peroxide to clean stains and apply the solution to your dog's fur. If you're not comfortable using peroxide on your dog's face, you can try a mixture of boric acid powder and cornstarch instead. Let the mixture dry for at least a couple hours and then rinse your dog's fur thoroughly with lukewarm water. Ensure these solutions do not make contact with your dog's eyes.
- Mix milk and peroxide in equal amounts. Make a paste by adding in cornstarch and allow the mixture to set for four hours. You can use this preparation to wash and condition the fur of your dog.
- One product that has been used by breeders and exhibitors to remove tear stains is Diamond Eye Tear Stain Remover. This clears up the staining and also keeps the skin under the eye healthy.

Preventing Tear Stains

The first, and most obvious method, is to gently wipe any sleet or debris from your dog's eyes with a damp cloth. You can use eye wipes especially made for dogs.

Antacids that contain calcium can also be fed to the dog. Such a product is Tums, which can change the dog's pH balance and reduce yeast.

One home remedy that you can use to inhibit the growth of bacteria and yeast is to mix a teaspoon of apple cider vinegar with your dog's drinking water.

If your dog's staining is a result of a genetic 'fault', then eye duct surgical procedures to increase tear capacity may be required; ask your veterinarian.

How Diet Can Help With Staining Issues

Your dog's diet goes a long way in preventing tear stains. Boost your dog's immune system by feeding her healthy, natural food. If your dog has a healthy immune system she will likely not encounter these infections. Feed your dog high-quality food that is devoid of artificial flavors, colors or preservatives.

Cataracts

Cataracts are often associated with older people rather than with dogs. However, dogs can develop cataracts and frequently do. A cataract is the clouding and loss of transparency of the lens. Cataracts can lead to blindness and are fairly common in old dogs. Cataracts are usually accompanied by other signs of aging such as arthritis of the joints and a general slowing down of the metabolism.

Cataracts most commonly develop with age, but sometimes they can occur after trauma, as a consequence of glaucoma (high pressure in the eye) or diabetes, and due to inherited conditions. So, if your dog develops cataracts, have her tested for diabetes.

Cataracts occur when the levels between water and protein in the dog's lens are disrupted. In a healthy eye, the lens consists of 66% water and 33% protein. If the eye's flushing system begins to fail, the eye will not be able to remove any of the excess proteins. This excess protein makes the lens appear cloudy.

How do you know if your dog has cataracts?

Many dog owners notice that their dog's eyes start to look increasingly white and cloudy. Your dog may start to walk into objects and be reluctant to go out in the dark, as the first thing that deteriorates with cataracts is night vision. In many cases, it is the vet who notices the development of cataracts at a regular check-over.

Can you prevent cataracts?

Keeping your dog at a healthy weight and feeding her a good diet are the only ways to help prevent cataracts. Obesity can bring on cataracts through diabetes mellitus which is a common cause of cataracts.

Free radicals are also thought to accelerate the development of cataracts. Anti-oxidants (found mainly in vitamins) can help prevent damage from these radicals that circulate in our bodies.

What can be done about cataracts?

Cataracts usually develop gradually with old age and can lead to blindness in one or both eyes. Many dogs cope well with the condition. Since dogs don't rely solely on their vision to get around and have their smell to guide them too, blindness does not have to be disabling for a dog. If you make sure that you don't change the furniture around and take some extra care when you walk your dog, you will be amazed how well dogs can cope with blindness. Children should exercise caution when dealing with a dog with cataract as they can startle the dog.

Cataract surgery is an option, especially in severe cases, but it can be expensive.

Conjunctivitis

Conjunctivitis is the inflammation or infection of the conjunctiva in the dog's eye. The conjunctiva is the thin membrane that covers the inside of the eyelid. The condition makes the dog's eye appear red. Conjunctivitis is often called pink eye, especially if the entire eye is red. Discharge can accompany conjunctivitis and this can be clear, brown or yellow-greenish in color. Common causes of conjunctivitis are allergies, as well as bacterial and viral infections.

How do you know your dog has conjunctivitis?

You might notice that your dog's eyes appear red and show some discharge. Conjunctivitis can be very agitating and painful to your dog.

Many dogs will paw at their eyes and/or rub their face on a variety of surfaces to eliminate their discomfort.

If the conjunctivitis is due to an infection, the eyes may close up and stick shut, excreting a yellowish or green discharge. Allergic conjunctivitis will often have a thin and clear discharge that is very similar to the dog's natural tears.

What can be done about conjunctivitis?

When your dog shows signs of conjunctivitis, take her to the vet. Conjunctivitis is very irritating and because the eyes are sensitive, it should be treated immediately to avoid further damage. If left untreated, conjunctivitis can also affect other parts of the eye and this can become quite serious and difficult to treat.

Your vet will give the eyes a thorough examination. In serious cases, she might take a swab and send it to a lab to find out what causes the inflammation. If necessary, the vet will prescribe an ointment that might contain antibiotics and/or steroids to help reduce the inflammation fast. Many eye ointments have to be applied often, sometimes 3–5 times daily, to achieve the desired effect.

Dry eye

Dry eye is fairly common in dogs. It occurs when the eyes don't produce enough tears to keep the eye lubricated. In most cases, dry eye is immune mediated. This means that the body attacks its own cells, in this case the cells that produce tears. Dry eyes are often very itchy, irritated and painful. The dog may feel the need to keep her eyes closed and feel very depressed with her condition.

How do you know that your dog has dry eye?

Your dog may develop a thick, sticky, yellow discharge. She might appear uncomfortable and rub her eyes on furniture or on the floor. To diagnose dry eye, your vet will perform a simple 'eye strip' test. A thin test strip is applied to the eyes. The strip measures the amount of tears the dog produces within a specified period of time; insufficient tears are a sign of dry eye. Tears have an antiseptic quality and so poorly lubricated eyes are also prone to infection.

What can be done about dry eye?

To treat the condition, you will have to administer eye drops regularly (5–10 times daily) to lubricate your dog's eyes. If an infection is present, your dog might also need antibiotic eye drops for a period of time in addition to the lubricant. In addition, cortico steroid eye drops and eye drops containing cyclosporines (an immuno-suppressant) can help ease the condition. Surgery can be a permanent solution to the problem.

Can you prevent dry eye?

In one word – no. There's nothing you can do to prevent this condition other than avoiding dog breeds that are commonly susceptible to this condition, especially Yorkshire Terriers.

Eye lash and lid problems

There are many different lash and lid problems from which dogs can suffer. These problems can range from the edges of the eyelids being rolled inwards (entropion) or outwards (ectropion), to ingrown lashes. Eye problems need to be evaluated by a veterinarian, and should not be ignored.

How do you know your dog has an eye lash or lid problem?

Lash and lid problems generally cause great discomfort and irritation – infections, redness and inflammation may be present. Your dog's eye may be pink in color and discharge may also be present. Most dogs will rub or scratch their eyes, show frequent blinking or winking, and rub their eyes on objects such as blankets and furniture. They may also try to bury their heads in your hands and make pleasurable moans when you rub their eyes gently.

What can be done about eye lash or lid problems?

It is important to remember that your dog is going to be extremely uncomfortable if anything is bothering her eyes. So, if you suspect your dog to have some type of lid or lash problem you should take her to the veterinarian immediately. In many cases, surgery can correct the issue permanently.

Caring for Your Dog's Coat

No matter what kind of dog you have some grooming of their coat will be required. However, different dogs will have different grooming requirements, depending on their coat type.

Grooming requirements for different coats

Short, smooth coats generally require the least amount of time and attention. Medium-long coats require more care, such as brushing and bathing. And dogs with long coats usually require the most brushing, combing and care.

Smooth coated dogs

If you have a dog with a short, smooth coat you will most likely need a good brush, such as a boar bristle brush, curry brush or a hound glove. A hound glove or curry brush removes dead hair and gives your dog's coat a good glossy shine. As for a bristle brush, it is excellent for most types of dogs and is useful to smooth out a dog's coat.

You may also need to use a pair of scissors to trim hair between the toes, around the ears or along the bottom of the tail, just to tidy your dog's appearance. For bathing you can use a good dog shampoo and a dollop of conditioner. No blow drying is necessary - just towel dry your dog.

Short-haired dogs

Short-haired dogs are considered 'wash and wear' dogs because you can simply bathe and towel-dry them.

Medium coated dogs

For a dog with a medium coat, such as a Border Collie or an English Springer Spaniel, more grooming will be necessary. You will need to brush your dog several times per week to keep the hair from tangling or matting. You will require a good brush, such as a boar bristle brush; a good comb, such as a Greyhound comb; and a pinbrush to separate the dog's long coat and brush it carefully.

With a medium or long coat it is always best to dampen the hair before you brush it with the pinbrush.

You can use a detangler or mix a small amount of conditioner in a spray bottle and lightly spray it over the long hair before brushing. This will keep the hair from breaking off when you brush it.

For bathing you should look for a shampoo that has conditioners in it. Make sure that you rinse thoroughly. You should then apply a small amount of conditioner and let it sit for a couple of minutes before rinsing thoroughly. You may wish to blow-dry a dog with medium hair to encourage the hair to lie properly and look good. You can brush the hair while you blow dry.

Long-haired dogs

If you have a dog with long hair, such as a Maltese or an Afghan Hound, then you will be spending more time grooming your dog. A dog with long hair needs to be brushed daily to keep the hair from matting and to keep it looking good. You will need a good brush, such as a boar bristle brush; a good comb, such as a Greyhound comb; and a pinbrush to groom a longhaired dog. Always make sure that you dampen your longhaired dog's coat before brushing to prevent the hair from breaking. You can use a detangler or put some conditioner in a spray bottle and mix with water then lightly spray over your dog's coat before brushing. For dogs with long hair it is best to brush your dog in sections and brush down to the skin to make sure that no mats are missed. You may want to invest in a grooming table since your dog will be spending a lot of time being groomed. You can teach your dog to lie down on her side to make grooming more comfortable for both of you.

A good brush for long haired or curly haired breed is the slicker brush. The slicker brush is made up of tiny wire bristles very close together. While this type of brush can be very harsh, it is essential for some dog's coats. When used properly, the slicker brush readily removes dead hair and matting.

Choose a shampoo that will condition your dog's coat and rinse thoroughly. Use a good conditioner and let it sit on your dog's coat for several minutes, especially the ends of the coat where the coat may come in contact with the floor. Rinse thoroughly. You should plan on bathing your dog at least once a month. You will probably need to use a blow dryer to help speed the drying process. Again, it will be more comfortable for you and your dog if you teach your dog to lie on her side while you blow dry her hair. Be sure to dry your dog everywhere to avoid leaving damp spots that could become itchy or turn into hotspots for your dog.

Wirehaired coats

Some breeds have wirehaired coats. These coats can be harder for pet owners to groom; you may need to take your dog to a professional groomer for clipping. If you wish to groom your wirehaired dog yourself you will need a terrier palm glove to remove loose dead hair, a comb, a good pair of scissors, and clippers or stripping knives, depending on how you intend to groom your dog. You can learn to clip your wirehaired dog's coat yourself and talking to people who groom their dogs. You can also learn to hand strip or 'roll' your wirehaired dog's coat. This is the process of plucking out dead hairs as they become straggly to keep your dog looking neat and tidy. Terrier coats are not conditioned the same way as other breeds. They are not intended to be soft. Instead, they should be harsh and crisp in order to be weather-proof. You will need to look for shampoos and conditioners specially-designed for terrier breeds. Bathe these dogs as little as possible. Using clippers on a terrier coat will make them soft instead of hard. Hand stripping and rolling the coat keeps it hard and in good condition.

Combs

Dog combs come in three versions: fine, medium and wide-toothed. Combs are useful to detangle hair and to help remove fleas and their debris. You can always use a spray on detangler to assist with removing tangles. Dogs with silky soft hair, fine hair or medium texture need a fine or medium comb. For coats that are dense and very thick, you should use a wide-toothed dog comb. To combat matting on curly and long-coated breeds, you can use a coat rake, mat comb or mat splitter.

Bathing your dog

Washing your dog is not always an easy task, therefore it is very important that you make this as easy as possible for yourself and your dog. Some dogs love water, others loathe it and some will just tolerate it.

Bath essentials

Firstly, make sure you have the right equipment ready for the bath: dog shampoo, a plastic water jug (you can use a plastic milk carton), face wash cloth and a towel. Also, have some treats ready. You may also like to have a bathing brush handy. A gentle bath brush can give your dog a nice massage during bath time, as well as stimulate your dog's skin and hair follicles.

Before going any further, let's talk about shampoos. There are many types on the market: there are shampoos specifically formulated to combat fleas and ticks, 'no tears' shampoos as well as tear stain removers, shampoos that are hypo-allergenic, scented shampoos that help combat pet odor, shampoos that give extra body (especially good for double-coated breeds such as the Newfoundland), natural organic shampoos with oatmeal (great for soothing irritated skin), shampoos that brighten white coats, shampoos that enhance the color of darker coats and shampoos for senior pets who may have sensitive skin.

There are many dog shampoos and conditioners on the market so it may be a little daunting to choose a quality shampoo and conditioner for your pet. When looking for a shampoo, go to a reputable pet store and ask the clerk what they recommend. They usually have the dogs' best interests at heart. However, it's best to be armed with good information. Here are six quick tips to ensure you are picking a quality shampoo and conditioner for your dog:

1. Never use human shampoo or conditioner on a dog.
2. Look for a shampoo with a pH that matches your dog's breed. Some shampoos and conditioners for dogs have formulations similar to human products. Although this might seem okay, in fact your dog's skin pH is higher than a person's, so her hair and skin needs are different. A dog's pH varies from 6.2 to 8.6 depending on the breed. If you use a product with a high pH you run the risk of drying out your dog's skin.

3. Look for formulations that have oatmeal and aloe vera as well as omega 3's because they moisturize your dog's skin.

4. Homeopathic ingredients such as spearmint, peppermint, emu oil, jojoba oil, oat, geranium and lavender are also great ingredients in pet hair products.

5. Products with zinc (zinc pca for puppies) are great as they help kill germs and bacteria on the dog's skin (which can cause itchiness and odor).

6. Dogs can also benefit from tea tree oil as this is a soothing agent.

Next, if you are bathing your dog in a sink or bathtub, make sure you use a rubber bath mat to prevent the dog from slipping and getting injured. These can be purchased from any hardware store.

Bath procedure

Before placing your dog in the bath or sink, make sure the water is tepid. Tepid water is between 20 and 30°C (between 68 and 86°F).

In order to place your dog safely in the bath, cradle the dog from underneath, making sure you have a firm hold on her upper and lower torso.

Use the plastic water jug to pour water over the dog. Then, thoroughly and gently massage shampoo into your dog – starting from the top and working your way down to the legs and tail.

When bathing your dog, avoid pouring water on her face and ears. Dogs loathe having water splashed and poured over their face. I am only speculating, but I believe the action of pouring water over your dog's face can trigger panic as a result of an instinctual fear of drowning.

Also, you want to avoid getting water inside your dog's ear canal – after the bath it's always a good idea to check inside your dog's ears. If your dog is not prone to ear infections, then this won't be a big deal: just monitor your dog over a couple of days for signs of ear irritation. If your dog is prone to ear infections and you notice you have accidentally splashed water into her ears, then clean them.

If your dog frets or attempts to leave the bath, hold your dog firmly and give treats so the dog becomes occupied with eating. You can also bring a toy into the bath, if that helps.

Thoroughly rinse your dog. Thorough rinsing to remove all shampoo and conditioner is very important, otherwise your dog may have to endure uncomfortable itchiness. Also, if you do not rinse thoroughly, you'll notice the shampoo leaves a fine powdery residue - it will look as though the dog has dandruff!

For the face and ears, use a small wash cloth. Wet the wash cloth and place the tiniest amount of shampoo on it. Then gently wipe your dog's face. Rinse the wash cloth thoroughly and wipe down your dog's face and ears again.

After you are done, gently lift the dog out of the bath in the same way you lifted her into the bath. Use the towel to dry her. If your dog has long hair, you may want another towel as a backup since it will get drenched quickly.

It's natural for dogs to shake off excess water – so expect to get wet!

A bath once a month is enough. If you wash your dog too often, you will strip the natural oils from your dog's skin which could lead to skin irritation and possibly other skin problems.

If your dog becomes stinky between washes, you can always use talcum powder or a waterless shampoo (available at pet stores) to deodorize your dog. Lightly shake some powder over your dog's back and legs then brush it through. Make sure you cover your dog's eyes when you apply the talcum powder.

Chapter 4
Games to Keep Your Dog Happy and Allow You Both to Bond Beautifully

Dogs that are not occupied on a daily basis often find their own outlets. These outlets (such as digging or excessive barking/howling) can be quite destructive and frustrating for you as an owner! A key strategy for staving off boredom and problem behavior is keeping your dog occupied. There are many ways you can do this and we will look at each of these options in turn.

In this chapter, I'll explain:

- How to organize your dog's daily routine and environment so your dog is confident and happy.
- How to cater to your dog's particular exercise needs, depending on her breed.
- Fun games and toys that will stimulate your dog and excite her curiosity.
- How to keep your puppy happily occupied while you are away from home.

Organize Your Dog's Day

Dogs are creatures of habit. They derive security and balance from knowing they can rely on certain things to happen on a regular basis. I have noticed that dogs with haphazard or unpredictable schedules tend to be a little more restless and insecure than their confident counterparts.

Consider scheduling the following activities as part of your dog's day:

- Ensure that your dog eats at the same time every day. For details on feeding schedules for puppies throughout their development to adulthood, see Chapter 2: Nutritious Food for a Well-Fed and Healthy Dog.
- Play with your dog. The best times to play with your dog is when you have been home for at least an hour. Do not play with your dog as soon as you arrive or just before you leave home. If you do, you may accidentally encourage your dog to develop separation anxiety. This is because your dog will fret in your absence, waiting for the moment you return so play can begin!
- Train your dog once a day. The best time to train your dog is just prior to a play session. In this way, you can use play as a reward. Remember, though, that training should be as fun as play. Training is great for both your dog's mind and her physical health. It's been said that training uses three times more energy than exercising, so training is a great way to tire out your dog! Training in short bursts and ranging in length from just one to fifteen minutes a day can help alleviate a dog's boredom. For puppies, I recommend that sessions are no longer than five minutes each. I'll explain how to teach your puppy various commands in Chapter 7: How Can You Train Your Dog to Be Remarkably Obedient and Wonderfully Well-Behaved.
- Walk your dog every morning. Following her full course of vaccinations, your puppy can be taken outdoors. Puppies tire easily and so walks should be short. As your puppy grows, you can gradually increase the length of walks. By taking your dog for a walk in the morning, your dog will be more contented during the day and less likely to engage in destructive activities such as digging and barking.

Although I advocate a daily schedule for dogs, it is important to ensure that your dog experiences nice surprises and variety too. Impromptu visits to dog parks, beaches and friends' homes can contribute to your dog's overall mental wellbeing. Surprise treats and playtime are also recommended. These, along with certainty around when to expect food, exercise and training will give your dog confidence in the pack's ability to survive.

Train and Task Your Dog

Giving your dog tasks to do for you is a great way to give your dog significance. Dogs love to serve their pack and so relish the idea of undertaking tasks. Tasks can include simple obedience, such as sit and stay. Regular training - even for tasks with which your dog is already familiar – gives your dog an opportunity to 'please' you. I have included some training exercises in this guide that you can use to help you assert your role as pack leader and give your dog some much needed positive reinforcement. Other tasks that can be given to your dog include fetching various items or carrying a backpack during walks. Never use a backpack on a growing puppy or adolescent. Once your dog reaches adulthood, you can place some weights (such as small plastic bottles filled with water) in your dog's backpack. The weights should never exceed more than 10% of your dog's body weight. Your dog may not like the idea of carrying a backpack at first, so help your dog become familiar with the backpack by allowing her to wear it without any weights at first. As your dog accepts the backpack, add weights in small increments.

Your Dog's Exercise Needs

Regular exercise is an essential part of dog ownership. Different dogs have different exercise requirements. The American Kennel Club recognizes some 160 breeds of dog and there are an estimated 400 different breeds of dog in the world today. That means that there can be enormous differences between dogs, ranging from the tiniest Chihuahua to the largest Mastiffs and Great Danes. It's clear that different dogs should have different kinds of exercise. Forcing a Pekingese to jog or swim could be very harmful, while more athletic dogs need regular exercise to stay fit and happy.

Here are some exercise suggestions for some of the different groups of dogs recognized by the American Kennel Club. Groups are arranged according to a breed's original purpose so many of the dogs in these groups should be able to do at least some of the kinds of exercise suggested.

Exercise for sporting breeds

Members of the Sporting group include the Pointer, the Retrievers (Golden, Labrador, Flat-Coat, Curly-Coat and others), Setters, Spaniels, the Vizsla and other naturally athletic breeds. These dogs were all originally bred to find birds and other game. Depending on the breed they can point, set, retrieve or flush out birds. Most of these dogs are capable of running for long distances, though some (such as the Clumber Spaniel) move at a slower pace. Many of these dogs, such as the Retrievers, particularly enjoy water sports.

You can provide good exercise for these dogs by taking them jogging or biking with you. They are ideal dogs for people and families with an active lifestyle. Most of these dogs are also very good at agility and other dog sports such as flyball and frisbee or disk throwing. Many of them, such as Labradors and Goldens, also excel at all kinds of obedience training. Many kennel or dog clubs provide hunt tests for sporting dogs which are a lot of fun for these dogs since they are able to exercise their natural instincts and get plenty of exercise in the field.

Exercise for herding breeds

Members of the Herding group include the Border Collie, the German Shepherd Dog, the Belgian Malinois, the Collie and the Corgis. The members of this group are acknowledged to be some of the most intelligent of all dogs. They were originally used to herd flocks of sheep, goats and other animals, or to drive cattle. They have strong herding instincts and may herd kids and other pets unless taught not to do so. They usually enjoy training and work to a great degree.

Herding dogs usually need plenty of exercise. They are extremely intelligent dogs and if they don't have enough exercise they can become very bored and unhappy in the home. They are brilliant at agility, flyball and other dog sports. Many of these dogs, such as the Border Collie, the German Shepherd and the Malinois, can also excel at obedience training. Some of these dogs are very versatile because of their intelligence and can be trained to do many things such as working as guide dogs, bomb detection dogs or doing other jobs. When possible, many of these breeds also enjoy herding work. You can even teach some of these dogs to play soccer and other games with balls that involve pushing or 'herding' a ball into a goal.

Exercise for hounds

The Hound group is divided into two groups: sight hounds and scent hounds. Sight hounds include Greyhounds, Salukis, Whippets and other dogs which hunt by sight. These dogs are all extremely fast and they love to run. Scent hounds work by scenting their prey. They have great noses. These dogs include the Bloodhound, the Beagle, the Foxhound and other similar dogs. They may work more slowly than the sight hounds but they excel at tracking their prey.

You can provide wonderful exercise for sight hounds by making sure that they get a good run several times per week. Dogs such as Greyhounds are usually couch potatoes at home and are very laid back, but they do need plenty of exercise. Take them someplace where they can safely run off-leash. Be sure it is a safe, enclosed area because once a sight hound starts running she probably won't return to you until she's tired, especially if she's chasing something. These dogs have a very strong prey drive. Sight hounds also love lure coursing which is a sport that allows them to chase a plastic lure on a wire. Open field coursing is another option for sight hounds, in which they are actually able to hunt hares in an open field.

With scent hounds you can enjoy the sport of tracking. Tracking allows the dog to search for items or, for advanced dogs, a person using her nose to find them. It requires a great deal of training and practice on the part of the owner and dog but scent hounds are terrific at this sport. Other scent hounds take part in hunting such as coon hunting or rabbit hunting. Dachshunds are also part of the Hound group and they take part in Earth dog events, going to ground after rabbits or squirrels.

Exercise for working breeds

The Working group contains many large breeds, including many mastiff-type dogs. These breeds have often been used as guard dogs or as livestock and flock guardian dogs. They include Akitas, Boxers, Giant Schnauzers, Great Danes, Komondorok and Newfoundlands. Although these are often very large dogs they don't always need a great deal of exercise. In many cases they are more content to stay close to home and care for their families.

You can provide good exercise for these large Working dogs by making sure that they are always well-trained. Working dogs are usually very intelligent dogs but they can often be independent-minded. Start training them at a young age and make sure that they have a good grounding in obedience. Working dogs can enjoy exercise if they have a chance to do the things for which they were bred. For example, the Newfoundland and the Portuguese Water Dog enjoy swimming and water sports. Samoyeds are very intelligent and agile dogs and can do very well in agility. Other dogs, such as the Boxer and the Doberman, will enjoy some all-around good exercise, such as going jogging with you.

Exercise for terriers

Terriers are often very active dogs so they appreciate exercise. These breeds include the Airedale, the Border Terrier, the Cairn, the Manchester, the Miniature Schnauzer, the Parson Russell (Jack Russell), and the Fox Terriers (Smooth and Wire). They were bred to hunt vermin such as rats and fox, going to ground after them if necessary. They are usually very brave dogs.

Terriers often excel at agility since they are small and fast. They can be hard to train but, with persistence, they can do well at obedience. Terriers may also enjoy participating in Earth dog events where they can dig and go to ground after small animals.

Exercise for toy dogs

Toy dogs don't usually require much exercise but they do need some daily exercise in order to stay healthy and sane. Exercise provides a good mental outlet for small dogs and improves their socialization. Many Toy dogs began with roles other than companion dogs. The Pomeranian can't pull a sled anymore and the Yorkie no longer hunts vermin, but these little dogs do appreciate having some real exercise.

You can provide good exercise for your Toy dog by taking her on a good daily walk. Do not force a Toy dog to exercise and don't allow her to become overheated. In most cases a good walk will provide sufficient exercise. Some Toy dogs may enjoy obedience or agility work, depending on the dog and the breed.

Exercise for non-sporting breeds

The Non-Sporting group is a catch-all group of dogs that originally had different purposes. These dogs come in different sizes and they don't really have much in common. Dogs in this group include the Poodle, the Chow Chow, the Keeshond, the Bichon Frise and the Bulldog. Exercise needs for these different dogs can vary greatly. For example, care needs to be taken that Bulldogs not over-exert itself. With its brachycephalic head and other physical traits, the dog doesn't need a great deal of exercise. However, the Poodle is a very athletic dog. Poodles began as hunting dogs and they are still very active, agile dogs. They are easily able to participate in agility, obedience and even work as retrievers and water dogs. If you have a Non-Sporting dog you should find out what kind of exercise is usual for your dog's breed and see if your dog is able to do that kind of exercise. Always start with a minimum of exercise and work up to more.

Stimulating and Fun Games

Dogs love play. It's an important part of their everyday life. Playing is a way of exercising, honing their fighting skills (with mock fighting) and bonding with others in their pack, whether dog or human. Many owners forget how important play actually is; owners often make the mistake of not providing playful outlets for their dogs. Regular play with you or a family member is important to your dog's wellbeing as it can help strengthen the dog-human bonds. Play with or without human company provides your dog with mental and physical stimulation (which helps to stave off stress or depression).

I recommend that you initiate the play routine instead of the dog. If your dog thinks she can demand attention from you at any time, then you run the risk of raising a needy, attention-seeking brat. Some games are great for general backyard shenanigans, while others are suitable during walks or as part of your dog's daily exercise.

It is easy to know when your dog is responsive to play. Dogs invite play by running around in big circles or adopting the classic play bow stance. Some dogs invite play by positioning themselves next to their owners and nuzzling or poking them. Some dogs will invite you to play with a particular toy or object by adopting a play bow stance with the toy in their mouths. Sometimes a playful challenge is set when a dog either lies next to, or stands over, a toy or other prized object.

Here are some great ways you can play with your dog and have fun together:

1. Fetch

Fetch is a great game you can play with your dog, especially since it requires less exertion on your part. Some dogs are born retrievers, whilst others have no inkling of what to do, so you may need to teach your dog the necessary skills. Before teaching your dog to fetch, it's important for your dog to know the sit and come commands very well. If your dog does not perform sit or come to a satisfactory standard, the job of teaching your dog fetch will be much more challenging. For information on how to ensure your dog performs obedience at an acceptable level see Chapter 7: How Can You Train Your Dog to Be Remarkably Obedient and Wonderfully Well-Behaved.

The following is a step-by-step explanation of how to teach your dog fetch. I have included all the steps as I am assuming your dog may have little or no inclination to retrieve an item; these steps will ensure that you have all bases covered. As you proceed through the steps, make sure your dog is consistently performing each step before moving to the next step. If your dog 'fails', then you have proceeded too quickly. All you need to do is return to, and repeat, the previous step until your dog is performing that step deliberately and consistently.

Start out by choosing a suitable item; it might be one that your dog loves such as a ball or squeaky toy. Or it can be a rope or obedience dumbbell (available at pet stores). Either way, make sure the item fits comfortably in your dog's mouth – if it's too big, the discomfort would override any joy your dog might derive from this activity. The idea is to make your dog as excited as possible about the item; some trainers refer to her process as making the item 'hot'. You make an item 'hot' by playing with it, tossing it up in the air, speaking in a high, excited voice, using your dog's name and saying: "Where's the ball? Who's a good girl? Where's the ball?" You can toss your dog a few treats, too, so she learns to associate the item with fun and excitement.

Next you should toss the item a little farther. Don't expect your dog to bring it back to you at first, but do encourage your dog to go after it. If she goes after the item and touches it you should praise her and give her some treats. If you keep associating the item with treats, your dog is likely to pick it up and you should give her a few more treats. You can start encouraging her to bring the item back to you once she starts picking it up. Don't chase her if she doesn't bring the item back to you. Once she starts carrying the item around you should hold off on the treats until she actually brings it back to you.

Once you are certain your dog is about to bring the item back to you, say "fetch" in an excited tone. If you say "fetch" when your dog is still in the process of figuring out what to do with the item, then you run the risk of the dog not learning to associate the command "fetch" with the actual act of bringing the item back to you. When your dog returns to you with the item, praise her and take the object from her mouth. Or show the dog a treat, and when she drops the toy as a trade for the treat, say "give".

When teaching your dog to fetch, you might encounter the following challenges:

- *"My dog does not let go of the object"* or *"My dog drops the object too far from me"* - Your dog should drop whatever she has in her mouth at your command.

For this to happen, make sure she is on a lead and follow these steps in order to train your dog to "drop it":

1. Play with the item until the dog has taken it from you.
2. Coax the dog towards you by jogging backwards. (Do not chase your dog, as this will only encourage the dog to run away with the item).
3. When you produce a treat, the dog is likely drop the item for the treat – as the dog drops the item, say "drop it".

- *"My dog does not pick up the object"* - If your dog does not hold the item in her mouth at all, then train your dog the "take it" and "hold" commands.

The steps to train your dog to "take it" and "hold" are:

1. Put the item in the dog's mouth and say "take it".
2. See that the item is in the dog's mouth and gently squeeze your dog's muzzle shut with your thumb over the bridge of your dog's muzzle and palm under the dog's chin. As the dog holds the item, say "hold".

There is another way you can teach your dog to pick up an item but it may take longer, so this method requires patience:

1. Make the item 'hot' (that is, irresistible to your dog) by playing with the item or teasing your dog with it.
2. Place the item on the ground and wait.
3. Whenever your dog looks at the item, say "good" and give your dog a treat. (Just remember that your dog may initially choose to look at you or the treats you have in your hand. That's okay, be patient and your dog will eventually look at the item again).
4. If you do this regularly your dog will quickly realize that she is being rewarded for giving attention to the item.
5. Your dog will eventually look at the item consistently and deliberately in order to get a reward. When this happens, hold off on the reward – this will encourage her to approach the item.
6. Reward your dog for getting closer and closer to the item.
7. Eventually your dog will choose to pick up the item. When she does so say "hold" and reward her. Repeat this last step to reinforce the "hold" command.

If your dog drops the ball far away from your feet, then there are some strategies you can adopt to encourage her to drop it closer. Coax your dog to run towards you, by slowly jogging backwards. Hopefully, this will also encourage her to drop the ball closer to you. Reward your dog if she drops the ball even a little closer than before. Keep rewarding closer drops and ignoring ball drops that are not closer than the previous effort. You can also stop the game if your dog drops the ball far away – your dog will learn that the fun stops when she doesn't play on your terms.

You can also play a little game called "drop it", where you get your dog sit (on a leash). Encourage your dog to pick up a ball or toy. Offer your dog a treat. As your dog lets go of the ball or toy, say "drop it" and give her the treat. Timing is important here – do not say "drop it" until the moment the dog allows the ball to leave her mouth. Once your dog has mastered this, you can gradually take small steps away and encourage your dog to come to you, before dropping the ball in front of you. You can then incorporate this game into fetch.

2. Hide 'n Seek

Dogs love to play hide and seek. This is an easy game to play. It helps if your dog knows a couple of basic obedience commands such as sit and stay. Put your dog in the sit and stay position and then go hide. That's it! You can give your dog the release command from afar and let her come looking for you. Or you can ask someone to hold your dog while you hide. If your dog is really clever, you can let her hide while you go searching for her. Dogs in training as tracking dogs have to play hide and seek with their handlers in order to develop search skills.

3. Tug of War

Dog trainers generally dismiss tug of war as a game that encourages your dog to challenge your leadership. However, what the experts don't tell you is that you can enjoy this whilst maintaining your status as leader of the pack.

The fact is that dogs enjoy playing this particular game with their owners and others in the pack. Dogs that play this do not necessarily use it as a way to challenge other pack members or their owner, and they certainly will not become competitive solely on the basis of playing it. It's fun and entertaining as it gives your dog a chance to bond with you and exercise their strength. It's also a good way to teach your dog several basic commands. You can use a simple toy such as a small rope to play.

Some dogs are more interested in playing tug of war than others but you can get most dogs to play if you wiggle the toy in front of them. You should praise your dog for taking hold of the toy to let them know it's okay with you.

If your dog gets over-excited and pulls too hard, or won't stop playing when you tell them to do so, you can simply stop playing. After all, it takes two to play tug of war and if you stop pulling the game is over.

You can teach your dog to "drop it" when playing tug of war. When your dog lets go of the toy you can praise her, offer her the toy again, or give her a treat as a reward. "Drop it" is a good command for your dog to know in case she picks up something she shouldn't eat or something dangerous.

How to play tug of war with your dog

If your dog gets overexcited and pulls too hard, or won't stop playing when you tell her to do so, you can simply stop playing. You can teach your dog to "drop it" when playing tug of war. When your dog lets go of the toy, praise her and offer her the toy again, or give her a treat as a reward. "Drop it" is a good command for your dog to know in case she picks up something she shouldn't eat or something dangerous.

Dogs love games of resistance - that's why many pull on a lead! Games of resistance such as tug of war should be played in such a way that your dog understands the rules and that you are always leader of the pack.

Rule #1: Always be the winner. This game can be enjoyable for your dog even when you win every time.

Rule #2: Make sure that your dog understands that you are the toy's owner. Even if you occasionally let your dog win, make her understand that the tug toy is yours. In other words, do not allow your dog to become possessive of the toy itself. The best way to retain possession of a toy is to put it away in a place that only you can access.

Rule #3: If your dog gets hyper-excited and yanks on the tug toy too hard, or won't stop playing when you command them to do so, you can simply stop playing. After all, it takes two to play and if you stop pulling the game is over.

Children and tug of war don't mix

Never let children play tug-of-war or chasing games with your dog as they see children as 'puppies' and will try to dominate them, which could lead to problems.

This game can be loads of fun for you and your dog as long as you set a few boundaries - so enjoy!

4. Tag

Other playful activities such as frolicking and playing tag mean that your dog gets plenty of exercise. Dogs love chasing each other – this is a common and fun game among pack members. When playing tag, always make sure that your dog chases you. If you chase your dog, then your dog may get accustomed to this. She may then run away from you whenever you move towards her, and this can be a frustrating experience if you are moving towards your dog in order to put a leash on her in a public area.

5. Find the Treat

This game can be really fun and rewarding for puppies. Grab three identical, lightweight and opaque containers. Place all three containers upside down on the ground and place a treat underneath one of them. Bring your puppy into the room and with your lead gently coax her towards the containers. As your dog explores the containers, say "Where's the treat?" When your puppy gets excited about the container with the treat, overturn the container so she can claim her reward! You can repeat this process, but make sure your puppy does not see which container has the treat. This game can be varied with more containers, spreading the containers out and using different kinds of treats.

Advanced Games

There are many other games you can play with your dog that are a little more advanced. This means there will be some extra effort required to train the dog to be able to play the game. Here are some more advanced games you can teach your dog:

Agility Training

Dog agility training is a sport in which a handler directs a dog through an obstacle course in a race for both time and accuracy. Dogs run off-leash with no food or toys as incentives, and the handler can touch neither dog nor obstacles. Consequently the handler's controls are limited to voice, movement, and various body signals, requiring exceptional training and coordination. Dogs can begin training for agility at any age; however, care is taken when training dogs under a year old so as to not harm their developing joints.

Dog agility is an international dog sport with many different sanctioning organizations and competitions worldwide. For most agility events there are two organizations involved – a club that actually organizes the event and a sanctioning organization. The sanctioning organization sets the rules, maintains competition records and issues titles or certificates when certain goals are met.

Backyard Agility

If you're interested in agility, you can set up a simple course in your backyard. A simple obstacle course can be quite a lot of fun for many dogs. This is a great way to develop a bond as your dog is learning to follow your instructions. You can make many obstacles from household and garden items such as: cardboard cartons, crates or blocks for jumps; a board supported by cement blocks for a raised walk; some bottomless barrels joined together for a tunnel; and a long board placed over a single cement block for a see-saw. You can easily purchase inexpensive items at the local hardware store. Just make sure all the items are stable, sturdy and safe.

Flyball

This is a race where dogs spring over a series of hurdles, run to a box, snatch up an object (like a ball) and race back to the starting point. The object of this sport is for the dog to finish this task in a minimum amount of time. The turn at the box can mean the difference between a win and a loss, so a lot of effort goes into teaching the dog to do this well. This event is just pure fun for many dogs, and it is open to all dogs, mixed breed and purebred alike.

Canicross

This game involves cross-country running while hitched to a dog. The equipment needed is a running harness, waist belt and a flexible line. In competitions there are more detailed requirements as to the length of the line. This is becoming a popular recreational activity for people who simply want to walk, jog, hike or stroll with their dog or multiple dogs without holding a leash. Joggers can run without compromising their stride while holding leashes.

Dog Soccer

For this game, a soccer ball or similar sports ball and a chair for the goal will do. For the goal, you can drape a towel around the legs of the chair, leaving one side open. The two likeliest ways for the dog to "kick" the ball are by using his paws or his nose. While some dogs are particularly skilled at using their paws to propel a ball with accuracy, the easiest way to train most dogs is to teach them to use their noses.

Dog Dancing

This is a modern dog sport that mixes obedience training, tricks and dance for creative interaction between dog and owner. The first step is to teach the dog how to work on both sides of the handler's body, not just the left side as in heeling. The trainer breaks the dance routine into phases with only two or three moves linked together. As they progress, these phases are linked together.

Earth Dog Trials

This activity tests the working ability and instinct of terriers. These breeds are natural hunters of vermin and other quarry that live underground. Earth dog trials involve man-made underground tunnels that the dogs must negotiate, while scenting a rat as the quarry. The dog must follow the scent to the quarry and then "work" the quarry, which involves vocalizing and scratching near the quarry's location. The sport is humane as the quarry is protected from any harm as the dog never gains any access to it.

Visit these websites for more information about dog events and activities:

- Dogs on Course in North America (DOCNA)
- Australian Shepherd Club of America (ASCA)
- Canine Performance Events (CPE)
- North American Dog Agility Club (NADAC)
- United States Dog Agility Organization (USDAA)
- United Kennel Club (UKC)
- Teacup Dogs Agility Association (TDAA)
- American Kennel Club (AKC)
- Jack Russell Terrier Club of America (JRTCA)

Toys and Puzzles

Dogs were bred to accompany humans and other dogs, however today's lifestyle does not allow people to have their dogs with them all day. As such, many dogs are left alone for long periods of time while their owners work or go about their day's activities. Dogs are naturally endowed with heaps of energy and they burn this energy with mental and physical stimulation.

Some dogs may sleep or rest in your absence because they are diurnal sleepers; they will then become more active when you return home. Some dogs will burn their energy with or without their owners help! These dogs, left to their own devices in a confined space such as a yard, will pace, chew or bark (and become anxious in the process). They are frustrated geniuses – they're clever, curious and therefore require different activities to stave off boredom.

Active, working breeds such as Huskies and Mastiffs are more likely to suffer boredom, however any dog is vulnerable. With this in mind, the following strategies have been designed to take into account an owner's busy lifestyle.

When a dog is home alone

The key to alleviating boredom when a dog is home alone is to ensure that the dog remains occupied with an activity for long periods of time. There are many ways you can keep your dog occupied:

Toys

To keep your dog occupied and entertained in your absence, you can provide her with a range of toys (indestructible toys are better). Don't leave the toys out for long periods as your dog will get bored with all of them. Rotate them daily. Use different toys for different activities: when you are away, when you are home, at the park or playing fetch. In this way, your dog will remain interested in all her toys and the toys themselves will remain intact for longer periods.

In the wild, dogs were accustomed to spending a significant amount of time looking for food. This instinct can be satisfied with interactive and food dispensing toys. These toys, such as a Kong, Buster Cube and Waggle, when filled with healthy treats such as canned food, kibble, cheese or meat chunks, can keep your dog occupied while you are away.

If you want to delay your dog's attention to it, then simply freeze the Kong or other toy and as it defrosts your dog will be able to pick out the treats!

Some dogs will eventually work out how to get to a Kong's stuffing inside, so you may want to make their job more challenging. You can do this by packing the stuffing tighter, or mixing cheese pieces or spread with food nuggets and then microwaving the Kong (inside a cup) until the cheese or spread melts. Let it cool to a safe temperature.

If you want to vary what you put inside your dog's Kong, then try any of these recipes concocted by dog trainers and vets. When trying these different recipes, always remain sensitive to your dog's stomach and don't introduce dietary changes too quickly.

Sand pit

A portable sand pit is a great way to occupy a dog that likes to dig. Bury toys and treats in the sand. Rotate the toys and treats so the dog is surprised at what she finds.

Chews

Many dogs have a natural tendency to chew and enjoy gnawing on something tasty. You can direct this behavior onto a large raw bone, rawhide and pigs' ears.

A huge marrowbone will also occupy your dog – but remove the bone once the knuckles have been eaten as the rest will grind down your dog's teeth. If your dogs have a tendency to bury their bones, consider a sandpit and train your dog to use it.

A raw egg (still in the shell) once weekly can initially offer a puzzle for your dog; once left in its dish your dog will eventually figure out how to get to the gooey contents! Don't worry about the shell – dogs stomachs are equipped to handle it.

Frozen goodies

Small frozen packs or ice-cubes of soup, bouillon (broth) and lactose-free milk can be placed in your dog's bowl before you leave on a long absence. These will defrost gradually, giving your pet a slow-release treat. Soups can be easily made with warm water, meaty chunks and vegetables. Vegemite or stock cubes can also be added.

Dog walker

A dog walker or pet minder is a relatively inexpensive way to have your canine friend occupied while you are away. These professionals can spend time with your dog in the backyard or nearby parks and walking routes.

Remember that if you are employing a dog walker or pet minder, tell them what activities your dog enjoys, so the dog will get the greatest benefit from the pet minding or dog walking service. Encourage the professional to engage your dog's mind with games and activities that are stimulating for your dog.

Noise

Some dog owners report that leaving the radio and TV turned on offers their dog some comfort, however this is not a cure for separation anxiety. Leave the radio on in a room with the door closed, to give the impression of someone being home.

Alternatively, videos showing life-size images of animals frolicking can be stimulating. Before using these methods for an extended period of time (that is, going out for the day), test them for short periods, and see how your dog reacts. Then increase the amount of time you spend out of the house on each subsequent occasion. If your dog finds the radio or TV over-stimulating you may want to discontinue using this method. After all, no one likes to come home to find a distressed dog and a living room in shreds, thanks to an over excited collie happily herding the dogs on the TV!

A room with a view

Does your dog have a view of an open space or the street frontage? Allowing dogs to watch passers-by can have a mollifying effect on them. Dogs that have limited access to a view may bark as they can get over-stimulated; providing your dog with a view for longer periods may settle them down.

A place to rest

A crate or kennel in the garden, in addition to helping with house training, can provide your dog with its own place to rest. You can also have a mat or space inside the house where the dog can rest. You can allow your dog access to the house in your absence with an electronic dog-door or flap. However, restrict the dog's access to certain areas if you are worried that she might destroy certain valuables.

Chapter 5
How You Can Enjoy Safe and Hassle-Free Trips With Your Puppy

Most pet owners will travel with their pets at times, whether it is to go on vacation, short trips or to simply make the occasional trip to the vet. If you anticipate car travel with your dog, then plan ahead and make sure your dog will be safe while she's in your vehicle.

In this chapter, I'll explain:

- Ways to ensure that car rides are comfortable and safe for you and your dog.
- How to manage car sickness.
- How to manage domestic and international air travel for your dog.

Safe Car Travel

Before you embark on a car journey with your dog, make sure you have the following items with you:

- Lead and collar
- Water
- No-spill water bowl
- Crate/Harness/Carrier

- Treats
- Wipes or cloths
- Recent picture of your dog
- Safety measures

Your priority is your puppy's safety, therefore consider how you will secure puppy in your vehicle. Ideally, your dog should always ride in the back seat or back area of your car. If you have no choice but to put your dog in the front passenger side (in a truck, for instance) be aware that dogs, like children, can get hurt if the air bag is deployed. Below are three options for keeping your dog secure in your car:

Crates and carriers

One way to keep your dog secure in your car is by using a crate. A crate can work very well for any size breed as long as the crate fits safely in your vehicle. Airline-approved crates, made of hard plastic, are usually safer than wire crates. They will provide some protection for your dog in case you are involved in an accident. Keeping your dog in a crate will prevent her from being tossed around in the car or propelled through the windshield. Also, in the case of an accident, a crate will prevent your dog (who may be disorientated or panicked) from exiting the vehicle and being struck by oncoming traffic.

Choose a crate that is large enough for your dog to be comfortable. She should be able to stand up and turn around. However, do not choose a crate that is too large as your dog can be tossed around inside it and sustain injury in case of an accident. Remember, crates can also be used for potty training – if you are looking for a crate that suits both your puppy's travel and potty requirements, make sure you choose a hard plastic crate. For more information about crates and how to familiarize your puppy with her crate, seeChapter 9: The Sure-Fire Way to Get Your Puppy Potty Trained In a Week. The crate itself should be secured with a seat belt in your car. For small and toy breeds, you may wish to use a soft-sided carrier. You can then use a harness or seat belt to secure the carrier in place so she won't be tossed around in case of an accident.

Harness

Another option when you are traveling with your dog in the car is to use a harness. This not only prevents the dog from becoming a missile in an accident but will also stop her from losing her footing on vinyl or leather seats. You might want to protect your car upholstery from dirty paw prints, puke and potty accidents by using a blanket, quilt or car seat covers. Earlier I mentioned bringing wipes or cloths, which will come handy in such an accident too!

Most harnesses work like a seatbelt for dogs, strapping over your dog's chest and holding her securely against the car seat, preferably in the backseat. Harnesses generally work best for medium and large dogs. Reward your puppy every time you place her in a harness. In this way your puppy won't fuss and will also come to love riding in the car and wearing her special seatbelt.

Dog barriers

A mesh or metal divider in your SUV or station wagon is a great way to confine your dog to the back of the vehicle. Many dividers are sturdy enough to withstand some impact in an accident.

Should your dog be allowed to hang her head out of the car window?

I don't recommend this. While it might be a fun activity for your dog, there is always the danger of your dog jumping out or airborne debris hitting your dog's face. Local traffic laws may also consider this illegal.

Keeping your dog cool and comfortable in your vehicle

Always ensure that the particular spot in the car where your dog (and crate) will be is well ventilated and shady. If unsure, try riding in that area of the car yourself. If you think the spot could do with more ventilation or shade, you can always have a small internal fan or window visor installed.

During trips

Take regular toilet breaks to avoid potty accidents in the car.

Car rides can be boring for all concerned! So make sure your puppy has access to her toys and that other passengers, especially children, do not tease or annoy the dog.

Can you leave your dog unattended in a vehicle?

When traveling with your dog, never leave her unattended in your vehicle.

It can be dangerous to leave your dog unattended in both hot and cold weather. Temperatures inside the vehicle can become much hotter or colder than the weather outside and your pet may be at risk of either hypothermia or heart stroke.

Exiting the vehicle

Always ensure that your puppy is on a lead before she exits the car so she does not have a chance to bolt. You can train your dog to jump out of the car on command too. To do this, follow the following steps:

1. See that your dog is in the car on a lead with the car door or hatchback open.
2. Have a friend gently hold your dog inside the car, or use the lead to keep your dog in place.
3. With frantic body language, coax your dog out of the car.
4. Just as your dog leaps out of the car, calmly say "out!" (or any other word of your choice).
5. Reward your dog.
6. Repeat the process until your dog learns to associate your command with the action of jumping out of the car.
7. Make sure the sessions are short and taught over a few weeks.

Do not train your puppy to jump out of the car if the car is too high for your puppy's size. If your puppy is forced to jump down a long distance, she may suffer an injury. You might like to invest in a ramp, which your dog can use to enter and exit your vehicle *(pictured)*.

Safe Motorcycle Travel

It is generally not a good idea to ride with dogs on a motorcycle.

Dogs are not always aware of the danger of jumping from moving vehicles and so having them unsecured on a motorcycle is exposing them to the risk of death or serious injury. For a safer ride on motorcycles, there are soft-sided pet carriers for small and toy dogs. They are similar to the airline-approved pet carriers which allow you to take small pets on planes. You can find soft-sided pet carriers for sale online and in some pet supply stores or motorcycle shops.

Managing Motion Sickness

The reason why some dogs get car sick is because they only go in the car when it's time to go to the vet. The vet can be a stressful place for a puppy, so she soon associates car trips with an unpleasant outcome and her anxiety causes nausea. Motion sickness can also be caused by stimulation inside your dog's inner ear. Many puppies suffer from some degree of motion sickness when they are small but, fortunately, they do outgrow it. However, some dogs will still suffer from motion sickness into adulthood.

If you have a puppy it's best to train her to like vehicles from the start so she doesn't develop, or continue to suffer from, motion sickness. You can do this by spending some playtime inside the vehicle with your dog without going anywhere, allowing your dog to get used to the vehicle when it's stationary. There may be odors or other things associated with the vehicle that can trigger your dog's nausea or anxiety; spending fun time together in the vehicle can help overcome the problem.

Then you can slowly introduce your dog to some short trips in the vehicle and give her treats. Make your trips together a fun activity. If you have a litter of puppies then take more than one puppy at a time so your puppy won't be scared or nervous in the car. Speak soothingly to your puppy in the car. Play music. Roll a window down part way if necessary to allow some fresh air into the vehicle. Secure your puppy properly in the car so she can't roam all over the vehicle.

If your dog gets sick in the car, make sure that you clean it up thoroughly. Your dog's sense of smell is very acute and if she smells this odor again it could make her sick again.

If your dog isn't able to overcome her motion sickness by getting used to riding in your vehicle then you can try some simple home remedies for dogs with nausea. Try giving your dog a few ginger cookies about half an hour before riding in the vehicle, or try some RESCUE® Pet (a natural, alcohol-free remedy that helps relieve stress).

If none of these suggestions help your dog then you should talk to your veterinarian about available medications to give her for motion sickness. There are several over-the-counter medications you can give to your dog but you should not use them without first discussing them with your vet. Dimenhydrinate (Dramamine®), meclizine (Bonine®), and diphenhydramine (Benadryl®) can all be used for pets to help with nausea. However, be sure to talk to your vet so you will know what dose to give. In severe cases, your pet may need a sedative prescribed by a veterinarian. Acepromazine and phenobarbital are commonly used sedatives for this purpose, but they must be used by prescription only.

Safe Travel Tips for Interstate and Overseas Flights

Flying with your dog can be a daunting experience for even the most experienced of travelers. Just as there are plenty of regulations and security measures for passengers, there are also lots of things to be aware of when you are flying with your dog. It's very important to take notes of all the regulations involved in flying your dog, to speak with knowledgeable representatives, and to confirm flight information. With good planning and attention to detail you and your dog will have a pleasant trip.

Domestic air travel

If you are flying domestic there are several ways for you and your dog to fly. If your dog is small enough and you are also flying yourself, you may be able to take your dog with you in-cabin in a small pet carrier. These carriers must be small enough to fit under the seat in front of you. Their dimensions should be about 8-10 inches (20-25 cm) tall, 17-19 inches (43-48 cm) in length, and about 15 inches (38 cm) wide. It's best to have a soft-sided carrier so it can be 'scrunched' under the seat with your pet inside while maintaining good ventilation on the sides and/or ends. Most of these carriers are shoulder-style bags so they are easy to carry. Airlines vary in how many pets they will allow to fly in-cabin but it's usually between two and ten. You should inform the airline that you will have a pet with you when you make your reservation. There is a charge for having a pet fly with you in-cabin.   It can range from about US$75 to US$200. Your in-cabin pet carrier will count as a piece of carry-on luggage.

If your pet is too large to fly in an in-cabin carrier then you will need to fly your pet as excess baggage. To do this, your pet will require a hard-sided, airline-approved crate. These crates are usually made of hard plastic with ventilation in the upper sides. They also have a metal grill door. The crates will also have a rim or lip along the middle of the crate. This is to prevent other crates and baggage from sliding into them and blocking the ventilation for your dog.

You will need to choose a crate that is big enough for your dog but not so big that your dog will be tossed around inside it in case of air turbulence. Your dog should be able to stand up easily in the crate without her head touching the ceiling. She should be able to lie down comfortably.

Check with the airline when you make your reservation to make sure that they can accommodate the size of crate that your dog requires. Some planes in smaller airports cannot accommodate crates that are size 500 or larger. If your dog requires a size 700 crate you can probably fly only on the largest jets with her. Most planes will be able to accept crates up to size 400 without a problem but make sure you talk to the airline representative or even someone in cargo to make certain that there won't be a problem accepting your dog's crate if it is very large.

If you have a large dog you won't be able to push her into a smaller crate in order to get her aboard the plane. Airline representatives are trained to check carefully to make sure that dogs are in appropriate crates. They will refuse to accept your dog and crate if they aren't satisfied that your dog is properly crated.

When you put your dog in the crate for travel you should also place some absorbent material in the bottom of the crate, such as a blanket or some newspapers. The crate should come with small plastic food and water bowls that snap onto the metal door. You should see to it that these are in place and have food and water ready to place in them at the airport. Complete most of your paperwork for the trip ahead of time. This usually includes a health certificate from your veterinarian stating that the dog is healthy and up-to-date on vaccinations (especially rabies). If your dog is flying during cold weather, you may need a statement of acclimation from your vet stating that your pet can fly in colder temperatures.

Preparing your dog for travel

You should start preparing your dog for travel a few days or weeks before the trip. Whether your pet will be traveling in a pet carrier or in a crate, you can help her get ready for the trip by letting her spend some time in the carrier or crate and making it a pleasant experience for her. Place treats in the carrier or crate. Let her go in and out as she likes. Leave the carrier or crate down in the floor for her so it's not a fearful object. By the time she's ready to travel, the carrier or crate shouldn't be something scary. She should be able to spend a few hours inside without becoming anxious. For more information about crate training, see Chapter 7: How Can You Train Your Dog to Be Remarkably Obedient and Wonderfully Well-Behaved.

Be sure to take your dog to the vet a few days before your trip to get her health certificate. Most states require a health certificate with rabies verification when passing from one state to another, although this isn't usually enforced when driving between states. However, the health certificate is required when you fly with your pet. If you are flying during cold weather, your vet should sign a statement saying that it's safe for your pet to travel at lower temperatures.

Most airlines will not accept brachycephalic breeds (short-nosed) for flights in the summer time, even with statements from a vet.

Be sure to have your dog's identification handy. Some people like to attach ID to their dog's collar in case the dog gets out of the crate. Other people are afraid that the dog may get the collar caught in the crate, so they don't put the collar on the dog in the crate. They tape the collar to the outside of the crate with the ID attached to it. Make sure that you are carrying your dog's paperwork with you, such as a copy of her registration papers, sales receipts, photos and other identifying papers in case she should get lost and you have to prove she is your dog. If your dog is micro-chipped, make sure that you have her microchip contact information with you and that it's up-to-date.

You will need to offer your dog a very light meal about four hours before you plan to fly. This is technically required by the airlines. But please don't force your dog to eat or feed her a large meal. This could make her become ill when she flies.

Be sure to get to the airport early but not too early. Walk your dog before putting her in the crate at the airport. This can help your dog avoid any accidents in the crate, especially if it's a long flight. If your dog is flying as checked baggage then it's good to get to the airport about two hours before your flight. You will take your dog to the check-in counter where she will be picked up and taken to a waiting area to get on the plane. Once you are on the plane you can ask the flight attendant to double check that your dog has been loaded correctly.

Be very careful about giving any kind of medication to pets that are flying, especially if they are flying as checked baggage or cargo. In these cases, there is no one around to check on your dog if she should experience any side effects from the medication. In most cases dogs that fly will sleep throughout a flight and will be better off without any medication.

Overseas Air Travel

If you are flying overseas with your dog, see the previoius section for information about crates and preparing your dog for travel. You will need the same type of crate for your dog and you willalso need an international health certificate from your veterinarian. If flying into the USA, your health certificate will also need to be endorsed by an APHIS-accredited veterinarian in order to satisfy the USDA. Some quarantine regulations will depend on the country you and your dog are visiting.

Whether you are visiting a foreign country or moving there permanently, it's a good idea to check with that country's consulate or embassy about regulations for bringing a pet into the country. For foreign embassies in:

- the United States, check here.
- the United Kingdom, check here.
- Australia, check here.

The following countries state that they have quarantine regulations regarding dogs:

- United Kingdom – 183 days; exemptions: dogs from Ireland, PETS qualifiers
- Hawaii – 30 days; exemptions: guide dogs
- Australia – 30 days; exemptions: dogs from Cocos Island, NZ, Norfolk Island
- Guam – 120 days; exemptions: dogs from Hawaii & UK
- Hong Kong – 30 days; exemptions: dogs from UK, Ireland, Australia, NZ
- New Zealand – 30 days; exemptions: dogs from Australia, Norfolk Island
- Norway – 120 days plus 60 in home
- Iceland – 56 days; exemptions: 42 days for dogs from UK, Norway, Sweden
- Japan – 14 days; exemptions: military allowed in-home quarantine

- Ireland – 30 days plus in-home 5 months; exemptions: UK
- United States – 30 day maximum following exam and vaccination; exemptions: immune animals 30 days minimum from vaccination date

If you are flying to any of these places with your dog then it's best to speak directly to someone in authority who can advise you about how imported pets are handled. For example, although the United States says that it has quarantine for animals coming from abroad, in fact, if a dog has been immunized in its country and shows no signs of illness, it may be brought into the country. Hundreds of thousands of puppies and dogs are imported into the USA each year under these rules.

The United Kingdom still maintains a quarantine period. However, for dogs that qualify under the PETS qualifiers scheme, they may obtain a pet passport and enter the country as visitors. Each year many dogs from other countries visit the UK and some even compete at the famous Crufts dog show. PETS allows dogs, cats and ferrets from other EU countries to enter the UK. Dogs from the United States are also eligible for a PETS passport. You can contact PETS directly for more information about obtaining a PETS passport:

- Telephone: +44 (0)870 241 1710 – Monday to Friday – 8am to 6pm UK time (closed bank holidays).
- Email: quarantine@animalhealth.gsi.gov.uk – Please enclose your postal address and a daytime telephone number.
- Fax: +44 (0) 1245 458749. There is also a minicom/textphone number for the deaf and hard of hearing: 0845 300 1998

If you are entering the UK from a non-qualifying country then your pet must spend six months in quarantine.

For more information about quarantine regulations for these pets in the UK you can contact the British government directly:

- Telephone: +44 (0) 1245 454860
- Email: quarantine@animalhealth.gsi.gov.uk – Please enclose your postal address and a daytime telephone number

If you are coming from a country that is required to go through quarantine, you can choose from different participating kennels around the country. It can be very costly to kennel your dog for several months such that you will not want to do this with your dog.

If you are planning to visit another country with your dog then you will need to check the specific situation in that country and find out their quarantine procedures. For example, if you are sending a dog to Australia from the United States, quarantine times can vary. Blood sampling is done for rabies and pets spend time in one of three government animal quarantine stations in Sydney, Melbourne or Perth. Check here for more information about quarantine measures in Australia.

For more information about different countries and their requirements you can visit PetFriendlyTravel.com.

Chapter 6
Safe and Fun Playtime With Your Dog and Children

Dogs and children can be great fun together, but sometimes they don't mix well. This is because children cannot 'read' dogs, and therefore children do not see the warning signs when a dog is distressed or agitated. Since children are unaware of what a dog is trying to communicate to them, a child might end up suffering a bite which could have been avoided if they had been able to heed the warning signs (such as a snarl, the baring of teeth or a nip). This is very different for puppies which quickly learn how to read their canine counterparts. When an adult dog bites a puppy, it is their way of exercising discipline – in other words dogs 'smack' with their teeth.

Direct and constant supervision is recommended when dogs are with young children. This chapter will empower you to teach your children how to interact safely with dogs. These tips are ideal for children who are aged 12 and under, and can be used as a guide for teenagers too.

How to Safeguard Your Children Around Dogs

Most dog owners have fond memories of having a dog as a childhood playmate. Seeing your child develop a special bond with your precious pet is great too. Although children and dogs generally do well together, it's always possible for accidents and injuries to occur. Many children are bitten or nipped by the family dog and studies have shown that the majority of these incidents could have been avoided. Parents need to take care to teach their children how to play safely, and interact, with dogs.

Here are some measures you can take to safeguard your children around dogs, whether they are the family pet or others' dogs:

1. Always supervise your children when they're around dogs. This is so you can separate them should the dog display any of the following signs of agitation or distress:

    *   Snarling
    *   Nipping
    *   Growling
    *   Cowering
    *   Wide, glistening eyes

2. Teach your children to be gentle with all animals and to respect them. This can be done by allowing children to participate in the training and care of the dog. Allowing your child to participate in structured play (such as a game of fetch) and obedience training goes a long way to ensuring that the child understands the responsibilities associated with dog ownership. It also allows dog and child to develop a strong bond. Make sure you give your children responsibilities that are age appropriate. Never give your child responsibility for controlling your dog in public until the child is strong enough to handle the dog.

3. When children are around, it is very important that a dog does not have access to toys (to which she has a strong attachment) or food. This is because dogs see children as lower in the pack and may 'discipline' the child (via a bite, nip, growl) in order to show the child that the dog has ownership over the food or toys.

4. Teach your child that the following behavior is inappropriate when interacting with a dog:

- Staring at dogs. Staring can be seen by the dog as a challenge, that is, an invitation to fight.
- Screaming and running away from dogs. This behavior can encourage the dog to treat the child as 'prey' and give chase. It can lead to a bite or an attack.
- Hugging or trapping a dog. Some dogs find this unnerving and may retaliate if they feel cornered.
- Hitting a dog or doing anything to harm or annoy a dog (including tail-tugging). A dog that is experiencing pain or irritation may retaliate.
- Bother dogs when they're sleeping. Some dogs can be quite grumpy when rudely awakened.
- Bothering the dog while she is eating. Some dogs are quite possessive and protective of their food.
- Taking things away from the dog. A possessive dog may discipline a would-be thief!
- Startling or scaring dogs. A dog that is startled or frightened may bite as a gut reaction, without realizing she is hurting a loved one.
- Approaching dogs from behind. Teach your child to call out to them so the dog knows who is approaching. This is so the dog is not caught unawares.

5. Make sure your child learns to never approach a strange dog, especially if it is unaccompanied by a person. If you and the other dog's owner are present, watch the dog's body language for defensive or timid behavior. If the dog seems wary, make sure your child does not approach the dog. Ask the owner for permission. Having said that, some owners may not realize their dog is uneasy, so it's up to you to make sure the dog seems safe. If unsure, err on the side of caution.

6. Have the child learn how to ask a dog's 'permission' before patting her. Teach children to say hello in a calm, confident manner and then gently put their palm out toward her and allow the dog to

smell it first. Then pat the dog under the chin. Dogs and puppies are not keen on being patted on the top of their heads.

7. You can teach your children about dogs by setting a good example for them in the home as you interact with your dog. Having a well-trained dog is a step in the right direction. If your dog is out of control and you are constantly yelling at the dog, then you are setting a poor example for your children about how to treat and interact with dogs.

8. If you don't have a dog but you still want to teach your children about dogs then, ideally, you could try to find a dog breeder who has a litter of puppies. Most dog breeders are eager to socialize their puppies with well-behaved children. Allowing your kids to play with a nice litter of puppies can be a good experience for them and a good introduction to dogs. It's probably best to stay away from dog parks with your children since dogs at dog parks can be very wild and rough. You may want to take your kids to a dog show. You can politely ask an exhibitor about petting a dog after they have shown their dog, when they aren't nervous or in a rush. Most dog show exhibitors are happy to talk about their dogs if you approach them at the right time. Plus, these dogs are well-groomed and well-behaved so they can give a good impression about dogs to your children.

Teaching Your Kids to Avoid Dog Attacks

Children should be informed on how to recognize the signs of possible dog attack and ways of avoiding them. In other words, you want to be able to acknowledge that a danger exists but not instill irrational fear. A matter-of-fact discussion about dogs should be enough to teach your child some basics about avoiding dog attacks.

Here are some guidelines you could give to your children:

1. Avoid strange or unfamiliar dogs. If a strange dog approaches, keep still and do not pat her or look at her.
2. Do not scream at a dog.
3. Do not run away from a dog. This is because dogs like to give chase. Some dogs see chasing as a game, but the child may think the dog wants to hurt them.
4. Do not make eye contact or stare into a dog's eyes. Some dogs don't like eye contact.
5. If a dog growls at you, leave the dog alone.
6. If concerned about a dog that is nearby, leave the dog alone and tell a parent or teacher there is a strange dog nearby.

Ask your school or vet about dog bite prevention classes.

Introducing a New Baby to a Dog

Never leave babies alone with a dog, even if you know and love the dog. Babies make strange noises and dogs can react oddly to them at times. Tragedies can and have occurred when babies have been left alone with the family dog. Exercise caution even when you are certain that the dog can be trusted.

Having said that, if you are bringing a baby home and are concerned that your dog may attack your infant, then please be assured that dog attacks on babies are rare. Parents are often worried their dog may attack the child as a result of resentment or jealousy, but this is simply not true. Dogs can misbehave as a result of rivalry in vying for the owner's attention.

It's important to note that there is no substitute for professional advice and that you should consult a dog behavior consultant if you are faced with the problem of introducing a new baby to a household with dogs in it. I strongly recommend a thorough evaluation by a qualified dog behavior consultant well before the baby's introduction so that appropriate measures and training can be undertaken. For sure, such evaluation can never predict the exact extent of the risk posed by the dog, but it can provide you with a clear idea of the risk factors and whether your dog represents a high or low risk to the infant.

During an evaluation you will be asked about your dog's:

- In cases where there is low risk, the dog behavior consultant can help you prepare for a smooth transition.
- Age, gender and breed.
- General activity level.
- Training history.
- Past socialization.
- Past history of predatory behavior with small animals.
- History of aggression towards people and dogs.

An evaluation is essential since even the most stringent training and precautions may not be sufficient to keep a baby protected from a dog that is considered to be a high risk to infants. In such cases, re-homing the dog prior to the baby's introduction would be ideal. Here are some factors that would increase the risk of a dog showing aggression towards babies and children:

- Lack of obedience training.
- Dogs that resist 'control', such as obedience training.
- Little or no socialization with children.
- History of aggression, nervousness or irritability with children.
- Overly sensitive or fearful of touch or hands.
- Fearful and unable to adapt to benign contact with children.
- A history of killing or stalking small animals.
- Dogs that are chained or kept outside.
- Dogs that become aggressive with only a low level of frustration.
- Dogs that react aggressively to being hugged, awakened or having their food or toys removed from their possession.
- Dogs advancing in age, or that have health issues that produce soreness, such as arthritis.

Socializing Your Puppy with Children

Just as you should teach children how to interact with dogs, you should also teach your puppy how to play 'nicely' with children. Learning to accept children should be part of a dog's early socialization. Some dogs seem to naturally enjoy being around children more than others. Golden Retrievers, Labradors and some other breeds are great with kids, while other breeds just don't seem to enjoy being around children as much. If you have children and you plan to get a dog, make sure that you consider breeds that are known to love kids.

Allow your puppy to interact with children often (and with supervision), especially when the puppy is between eight and twelve weeks old. Even if you do not have children, it's crucial that you allow your puppy to have good experiences with children so that she's not afraid when she comes in contact with children as she gets older. This is especially true if you plan to start a family within the dog's lifetime, if you anticipate that people will bring their children when they visit you at home, or if you expect to encounter children at the park.

Chapter 7
How Can You Train Your Dog to Be Remarkably Obedient and Wonderfully Well-Behaved

Without training, you'll raise a terror of a puppy. Similarly, half-hearted efforts at training will produce mixed results. Many owners are keen to devote time to training their dogs, but lack the know-how. This can make training a chore, which then results in the owner giving up. This chapter is a useful training resource for basic puppy obedience because you'll not only discover some critical ground rules and training techniques that will help you raise an obedient dog, but you'll also learn to nip problem behaviors in the bud.

Good quality obedience training is essential for your dog's psychological welfare and also ensures that dog ownership is a joy, rather than a burden. Obedience training is not just about getting your dog to do what you want, when you want; it's also an essential part of raising an independent and confident puppy. But formal obedience training is not the whole picture. There are many ways you can interact with your dog outside of training sessions – on a daily basis – that will make your dog secure and self-sufficient. This is especially important as your puppy learns to keep herself occupied and contented, even when you are away from home.

In this chapter, I'll explain:

- How to rate your dog's trainability.
- Basic ground rules that professional dog trainers apply that makes training easier.
- When and how to reward your dog so she is responsive and eager to learn.
- How to stop bad or undesired behavior without hollering, hitting or hurting your puppy.
- How to teach your dog to stand, sit, drop, heel and come.
- How to build your dog's confidence and ensure she is calm around people.
- How to ensure your puppy accepts strange noises, like lawn mowers, vacuum cleaners and vehicles.
- How to stop your puppy chewing your furniture and clothes.
- How to stop your puppy from nipping and biting people's hands and feet.
- How to stop your puppy from peeing herself, jumping or going crazy when she meets people.
- How to train your puppy to be self-sufficient so she won't fret and howl in your absence.

How Trainable is Your Dog?

Have you ever wondered what affects a dog's ability to learn new skills? It is very rare to find a dog that is not trainable to some extent, but the fact is some dogs are easier to train than others. There are eight factors to consider when looking at your dog's trainability.

1. Age

The old adage "you can't teach an old dog new tricks" is not entirely true; however, it is true that the younger the dog, the better her chances of picking up new skills. In fact, the optimal learning age for a dog is between 8-16 weeks. Dogs are also good learners prior to 8 weeks of age, but it is not advisable to separate a puppy from the litter during that period. Great breeders do expose litters to appropriate levels of noise and other stimuli so that the dogs learn not to fear certain sounds and activities.

When it comes to peak learning, dogs are like humans – our best learning occurs in the early years. While humans learn most before 7 years of age, puppies will learn things up to approximately 18 months that will stay with them for life. That's why early training is best.

The good news is that a dog's learning capacity is never shut off; older dogs can learn new skills, it's just that more time and patience is required. Having said that, very old dogs that suffer from dementia and other age-related disabilities may be quite difficult to train.

2. Temperament

Your dog's temperament is determined by her genes; her temperament cannot be changed. Generally speaking, a dog's temperament can be classified into one of the following three categories:

- Dominant
- Middle Pack
- Lower Pack

Dominant dog

This may come as a surprise for most people but it is the female dogs that are more likely to be the dominant dog in a pack.

Confident, dominant dogs stand straight with head level. If approached by other dogs, they stiffen in an upright pose. Generally, dominant dogs will not yield to other dogs – they won't lie on their back. These dogs will test their owners and tend not to be owner orientated. They will jump on you and walk ahead of you (unless they have been trained not to do so). Some owners fall into the trap of thinking that they should 'break' their dominant dog. This is irresponsible and dangerous to the dog's mental wellbeing. Dominant dogs simply require a firmer, more consistent and persistent training approach.

Middle pack dog

These dogs are generally friendly, easy going and compliant and, unless backed into a corner, will not fight other dogs. They will yield to the leader by lying on their back, cowering, lowering their head or darting. However, they will engage their subordinate counterparts by standing upright, stiff and head level. These dogs are generally great to train as they respond well to a confident and strong leader.

Lower pack dog

These dogs are focused on their owners and will always have an eye on them. They generally keep close by and respond quickly to rewards and corrections. They tend to submit to other dogs easily (by lying on their back, cowering, lowering their head or darting) as they do not want conflict. Thus, these dogs are very trainable, but watch out if they 'shut down', that is, totally withdraw from a training session, if the training is too harsh. Don't try to 'toughen' your dog with harsher training methods – this may stress her.

3. Breed

Generally, breed groups are known to have their own trainability factor. While the following are common characteristics for each breed, there will be variation within any breed depending on the individual dog.

Here are some basic characteristics for breeds and their trainability:

- Toys include Bichon Frise, Boston Terrier, Chihuahua, Chinese Crested, Italian Greyhound, Lhasa Apso, Pekingese, Pomeranian, Shih Tzu, Tibetan Spaniel, Yorkshire Terrier Papillon, Maltese Terrier, Japanese Spitz and Cavalier. Many prefer attention and reward for no effort and so will not enjoy obedience training.
- Terriers include Airedale Terrier, Manchester Terrier, Bedlington, Border, Cairn, Jack Russell, Kerry Blue, Pit Bull, Skye, Staffordshire (American & English), Australian Terrier, Black Russian, Irish, Fox (Smooth and Wire), Miniature Schnauzer, Miniature Pinscher, Scottish, Welsh & West Highland. These dogs can be strong willed and stubborn and off-lead obedience can be a challenge due to high distractibility.
- Gun dogs include breeds such as Pointers, Spaniels, Setters, Italian Spinone, Labrador, Poodle, Brittany, Weimaraner, Hungarian Vizsla and Large Munsterlander. These dogs tend to have a high trainability factor.
- Herding dogs include Blue and Red Heelers, Australian Shepherd, Bouvier des Flandres, Briard, German Shepherd, Old English Sheep Dog, Australian Kelpie, Bearded Collie, Border Collie, Belgian Shepherd, Cardigan Welsh Corgi, Giant Schnauzer and Shetland Sheepdog. Although these dogs can be quite excitable, they have high trainability.
- Hounds:
  o Sight hounds include breeds such as the Afghan hound, Borzoi, Italian Greyhound, Greyhound, Deerhound, Irish Wolfhound, Pharaoh Hound, Whippet, Rhodesian Ridgeback, Basenji and Saluki. They are considered to have a low trainability factor.

- o Scent hounds such as American and English Foxhound, Beagle, Dachshund, Harrier, Basset Hound, Blood Hound and Rhodesian Ridgeback. These dogs tend to have medium trainability factor.
- Flock guardians include: Anatolian Shepherd, Mareema Sheepdog, Komondor, Great Pyranese, Hungarian Puli and Kangal Dog. These dogs require extensive socialization and training – some make great family dogs while others may have difficulty adapting to urban life.
- Mastiffs include breeds such as American Pit Bull, British Bulldog, Bull Terrier, Boxer, Newfoundland, Neapolitan Mastiff, Staffordshire Bull Terrier, Bull Mastiff, American Staffy, Burmese Mountain Dog, Dobermann Pinscher, English Mastiff, Great Dane and Rottweiler. They are considered to have a challenging trainability factor as they require persistent discipline, fairness and consistency.
- Spitz-type dogs include Alaskan Malamute, Chow Chow, Keeshond, Samoyed, Chiba Inu, Akita, German Spitz, Norwegian Elkhund, Schipperke and Siberian Husky. They are considered to not particularly enjoy obedience training and they can be stubborn. They have a strong tendency to pull and can be challenging on a lead.
- Pariahs include Basenji, Dingo, Mexican Hairless, Canaan Dog and New Guinea Singing Dog. They are considered to have a low trainability factor because they are extremely difficult to motivate and are not interested in pleasing their owner.

4. Motivation style

When training any dog, it is important to find out what motivates her. This can be different for each dog. Generally, there are four things that can motivate a dog: treats (food), toys/objects, praise, and dislike of corrections.

With treats and toys, it can sometimes be a matter of what type of treat or toy your dog prefers. For example, my two terriers are not keen on tennis balls but they love their fluffy squeaky duck.

It's a good idea to experiment with toys and treats, to see which ones really excite your dog. It's also a good idea to rotate treats – dogs love to eat an array of foods. This will keep them guessing and interested. After all, variety is the spice of a dog's life too!

Some dogs thrive on praise and their owner's approval; other dogs really hate being corrected or experiencing their owner's disapproval. Surprisingly, you do not have to use harsh corrections – some dogs dislike the idea of their owner showing any sign of disapproval such as a growl or sharp "no!". You can use this to your advantage when training.

5. Health

A healthy, fit and active dog will more likely be responsive to training. Like humans, dogs have their days when they might be feeling a little 'off'. In such cases, the dog may not be as responsive to her owner's instructions. Luckily, this is temporary in most cases. Other longer term conditions, ailments and injuries might mean a dog is experiencing pain, lethargy or physical disability. This can significantly lower the dog's trainability, as she loses her capacity to follow instructions. Furthermore, the dog's desire to please the owner can be diminished.

On a more subtle level, poor diet and lack of exercise can affect a dog's health, even if only to contribute to a dog's general lethargy and malaise. Some dogs may even experience heightened anxiety or depression as a result of lack of enough fun family activity. It is therefore very important for owners to feed their dog a nutritious diet, exercise the dog regularly and give the dog regular opportunities to be trained, play with, and bond with her owners.

Surprisingly, dogs with hearing and sight impairments can still be trained. In these cases, the trainer should rely on training methods that focus on the dog's other functioning senses.

6. Training experience

Dogs that are familiar with training and the learning process are far more likely to pick up new tricks and tasks than those dogs with limited experience being trained. This is because a dog which has been trained regularly gets to know and understand the learning process and has some cognitive understanding that her owner is seeking new tasks for her. In this way, the dog immediately goes into 'learning mode' where she will experiment with her own behavior, with guidance from the owner, to work out what actions will get her a reward.

7. Owner's confidence and knowledge

Your energy 'travels down the lead' – this means that your own level of confidence is easily sensed by your dog. A confident owner puts a dog at ease; an unconfident one will affect the likelihood of training success. This is because dogs with dominant personalities will walk all over unconfident owners while nervous dogs will only continue to be at the mercy of their own insecurities when they sense their owner is also unsure.

Knowing exactly what you are doing is key to dog training. Plan your training sessions and be clear about what you will ask of your dog. Knowledge of good dog training techniques is essential in getting the best from your dog. This will also decrease your frustration as experienced owners know that it takes time and effort to teach new tasks.

8. Complexity of new task

Some tasks are relatively easy to train while others are naturally harder. Generally speaking, the more steps involved in a task, the higher the complexity. For example, 'sit' is easy to teach as the action of sitting can be completed in one movement. However, teaching a dog to retrieve an item is more complex as it involves teaching the dog four separate movements: walking to the object, picking the object up with her mouth, returning to the owner and then dropping the item at the owner's feet. Some dogs learn to fetch quite quickly, but for dogs that are reluctant to, or unfamiliar with, fetch, it can be quite 'complex' to train them because of the number of steps involved.

As you can see, the trainability of your dog depends on many factors. It is essential to be willing to work through any challenges you may encounter in training your dog in a calm and creative way. Apart from dire health and old age issues, you should be able to work through most challenges in order to train your dog well.

The Ground Rules of Dog Training

These basic ground rules for training your dog will allow you to get her to focus and obey without driving you to smacking or yelling at your dog. They will also ensure both you and your dog absolutely love training. As you apply these rules you will see a big difference in your dog's responsiveness to any new skill you introduce.

Here are my ground rules:

1. Ensure your dog is healthy, alert and pain-free. If you notice your dog to be unwell or tired, your dog is recuperating from illness or surgery or is in any pain, then abstain from training until she is well and alert again. There is *never* a reason for making a dog do something that causes her pain.
2. Train your dog at regular intervals. There shouldn't be a long period of time between sessions, especially when you are introducing your dog to a new skill. Ideally, training sessions should not be more than 24 hours apart. If you have been unable to train your dog for a couple of days, remember your dog may have forgotten what she has learned. In that case, you need to do your last session all over again. You can have many training sessions per day, as long as they're short, sharp and fun (see my other ground rules). This will make training fun, not a chore.
3. Train your dog in short spurts. All dogs, especially puppies, have short concentration spans. Training your dog for 2–3 minutes at a time is sufficient. With puppies, sessions can be as short as 10–20 seconds! This ensures that your dog's mind is fresh during

training. By dragging the session for too long, you run the risk of frustrating or boring your dog. Too many repetitions are a sure-fire way to turn your dog off training. Your dog will dread training sessions, weakening her desire to learn.

4. Always end the session on a win so you can spend some time praising, cuddling and playing with your dog. A 'win' is when your dog has done well and you have not had to correct her. In this way, your dog will have fond memories of the last session and will eagerly await the next one.

5. Train in a quiet, distraction-free environment. Teaching new commands in an environment with no distractions means there should be no other dogs, children, people or noisy things in the vicinity. You can introduce distractions gradually only when you are sure your dog knows the command well.

6. Make sure your family is on the same page when it comes to training the family pet. There is nothing more frustrating and confusing to a dog than to be subjected to different training methods, training schedules and corrections. It's probably best that one person in the family coordinates the training. This person can ensure all family members are agreed on how to train the dog (having them read this chapter would be a good start). It is also vital that all family members are kept in the loop in regard to the dog's progress in terms of what the dog is currently learning and at what stage she is at.

7. Have a starting and finishing cue for training sessions. Dog's love certainty – they like to know what is expected of them at any given time. These cues give them a clear distinction between training and other activities. By using a phrase to clearly signal the start and end of a session, your dog is given an opportunity to perform at her best; this is because she'll know she has a task to do. Dogs actually love working for their owners and these cues give them that satisfaction. I use "Are you ready?" to start a session and "Finished!" to end a session, however what you choose to say is up to you (as long as the same cues are used each time). It's always best to use the same physical gestures with

these verbal cues; I use arms out and palms up to signal "are you ready?" and arms crossed over my chest to signal "finished".

Physical gestures should always be used with verbal cues

"Are You Ready?"

"Finished"

8. Have the right equipment and training space. In this way, you won't be forced to cut the session short because you have run out of treats or cannot find a certain training tool. Later, I'll discuss what training equipment you'll need.

9. Be flexible. Training is a great opportunity for you to develop rapport with your dog. This bond ensures your dog is loyal and obedient. You develop rapport by really taking notice of what your dog is 'telling' you. If your dog is having difficulty getting a new command or is not responding to a certain training method, then change the way you teach. This may be as simple

as changing the types of reward or correction you are using, the length and timing of sessions or the type of training technique being applied.

10. Set your dog up for success. No one likes to fail often – it's demoralizing. Dogs are no different – if they feel they cannot please you, they will simply give up. When faced with constant failure (and punishment) some dogs will even shut down completely; this phenomenon is known as 'learned helplessness'. When a dog is constantly punished no matter what she does, the dog simply gives up. You set up a dog to win by using a good training technique (these are explained later in relation to each command) and by following these ground rules. One of the most important ways to set your dog up for success is to train 'incrementally'. This means teaching your dog a little at a time. For example, when you first train your dog the recall, you would ensure your dog is virtually in front of you. If you start with your dog on the other side of the yard, your dog is bound to fail.

11. Mindset is everything. A positive, upbeat approach to training will have a great effect on your training ability. Patience and confidence are essential. A confident owner will instill a strong sense of security in the dog. Never, ever show frustration or anger to your dog during training. By being angry you are signaling to your dog that you cannot handle the situation and your dog may shut down or play up.

12. Your dog decides her reward. When training your dog, carefully observe which type of reward your dog loves. Rewards are a dog's currency – different types of currency are valued differently by each dog. If your dog is a glutton, then use treats. Some dogs may go crazy for certain games like fetch or tug, while others long for affection. Choose the reward based on what your dog values most, not what you think is best. An advanced training technique used by professionals involves using a reward that your dog values, but then using an even more valued reward for breakthroughs or improvements in behavior.

13. Rewards should be given only occasionally once the dog has learned the skill. Initially, as you teach your dog a new skill, reward will be given every time she performs as expected or makes a small improvement in getting towards the desired behavior. As the dog masters the new skill, rewards are phased out gradually. If you drastically cut rewards, your dog will lose motivation. This is also the reason why many dog owners report that their dog refuses to obey unless there is a treat on offer – it is because the phasing out of the treat occurred too quickly.

14. Timing is key. Your rewards and corrections must be instantaneous. You have about two seconds to provide a response to your dog's behavior; after that she is unlikely to make a connection between the behavior and your response.

15. Only say the command once and make sure your dog performs the task. There is no need to repeat the command in an effort to get your dog to obey. Saying a command repeatedly, without the task being performed, teaches your dog that she can fob you off.

16. Always have your puppy on a leash during training. There'll be times when a leash is unnecessary, but this will be indicated in the training instructions. A leash is important as it is a way to keep your dog under control. Bear in mind that your confident handling skills, clear communication and technique all go a long way to making sure you have good control over your dog.

17. Don't expect too much from your dog. This means in each session the dog should only be exposed to one step at a time. If your dog succeeds in learning a new step, then give an extra reward and give your dog an opportunity to reinforce this step by having her do that particular step repeatedly over a few training sessions. Some owners expect too much from their dog. I see this often when owners try and train their dog the recall. Some owners expect their dog to come back when called in the park after they have taught the dog to come to them on a lead in the yard. But this is impossible as the dog is far away and has only learned to obey the recall in a small space such as a backyard.

18. When teaching a new command, have the overall goal in mind. Then break it down into steps – these steps will then form the basis of the smaller goals you will need to achieve in order to achieve the overall goal. Each command explained later in this chapter is broken down into steps so you will have a clear plan of how to achieve your goal.
19. When training, use clear communication. Use high tones for praise, neutral tones for commands and low, guttural tones to indicate disapproval. Each verbal command should be accompanied by a special hand signal. It doesn't matter what terms or hand signals you use as long as they are used consistently and come natural to you.
20. Always use a release word. A release word is the equivalent of giving your dog permission to be 'at ease'. By using a release, you are teaching your dog that she should stay in a commanded position until she is released or given another command. The release word can be anything, as long as you use that word consistently. I use the word 'free'. Some people use 'okay', but many professional dog trainers say the word 'okay' may cause the dog confusion because this is too commonly used in general conversation. A reward should only be given after you have released your dog (and your dog has performed the task as expected).

Reward & Punishment

In rule 18 above, I discussed using clear communication when training your dog. This means being obvious about whether you approve or disapprove of your dog's behavior. Rewarding your dog can be simply be a matter of using treats, toys, play and affection (see rules 12, 13, 14 above for more information about rewards).

What type of punishment you should use

Punishment is a way of expressing disapproval and should be applied humanely. This means the punishment should produce either annoyance, a startle, or some amount of discomfort – but certainly not pain. Studies have shown that hitting, kicking, slapping or using other corporal punishment on a puppy can cause behavior issues - such as aggression - later in life. Humane forms of punishment are:

- Guttural, gruff tones (such as a growl). These may be accompanied by a tug on the leash or a stare-down.
- clap or similar very unpleasant sound at medium to loud (but not deafening) volume.
- Boss grip (where the owner holds the dog's muzzle firmly closed). This is suitable for barking or mouthing issues.
- Isolating the dog (time out). This can be done by calling out 'enough!' and then firmly leading the dog to a secluded environment and then leaving the dog in that space for a short period of time. Two minutes is enough.
- Withdrawal of reward.

The level of punishment you apply should be proportionate to how robust your dog is. Using a distressing and forceful punishment on a timid, fragile dog is inappropriate and could induce crippling fear. Likewise, a soft punishment such as a low growl may have no effect on a sturdy, dominant dog. It's up to you to learn your dog's level of tolerance and adjust your punishment methods accordingly. If your methods are too 'soft' your dog will likely resume whatever behavior you are trying to avoid. Likewise, if you do not consistently punish unwanted behavior, your dog is unlikely to heed your sporadic efforts.

If you ever feel like using corporal punishment on your dog, remove yourself from the situation. I guarantee you'll feel better if you do. Usually, if a dog does not 'get' something, it's because you've missed something in your training technique. In such circumstances, review this chapter and see how you can improve your training methods.

When to use punishment

In the initial stages of teaching your dog a new command, there'll never be a need to punish your dog. This is because your dog is still learning the meaning of the command. Once it is clear that your dog understands what a certain word means, then you can introduce the punishment for non-compliance. You'll know when your dog has learned the association between the word and behavior when your dog has consistently performed the task about 10 times (over the span of several training sessions) without you having to coax the behavior. Therefore, especially during initial stages of training new behavior, you will be using rewards more often. When you introduce punishments, keep track of how many you have had to apply. If your punishments are more than one in ten, then your dog has not learned the meaning of the word. In this case, you'll need to go back to teaching your dog the command as if she is new to it.

Distraction-Proofing Your Dog

Initially, training sessions should be conducted in a quiet, distraction-free zone. Once you are certain your dog knows a command very well, that is, nine out of ten times in a row over the span of several sessions, you can slowly introduce distractions. Distractions can be simple things like you moving around, tossing a toy or treat and saying other words (that do not resemble the release word). Later, you can take your dog to the park and have your dog perform the tasks on a short, then long, leash. If your dog is having trouble with the distractions, then you have gone too far too quickly for your dog. Keep to a level of distraction that she can handle and proceed slowly. Remember to set up your dog to win!

Your Dog-Training Tool Box

If you are planning on getting a new puppy then it's a good idea to prepare in advance before bringing her home. You can make your first days together go much more smoothly with a little planning, and your new puppy will be much happier as a result.

Here is a brief checklist of the things you will need before you bring your new puppy home:

1. Your puppy will need a flat buckle collar and leash before you bring her home with you. A nice nylon collar and leash will do very well. There is no need to spend a lot of money on an expensive collar at this stage, nor to buy something leather. Your puppy will be growing quickly and will soon outgrow her first collars. Buy something that is practical and safe. You may wish to get a collar that is brightly colored in case your puppy wanders away from you. Something bright will make her easier to spot. Her leash should be about six-feet long. You'll also need a longer leash (about 20-30 feet long) which you can use when your puppy's training becomes advanced and you would like to do some distance work at home or in a public area.

2. Your puppy will need a crate for sleeping and house training. Even if you don't plan to have your puppy sleep in the crate on a regular basis, all dogs should be crate-trained. It is recommended that dogs ride in crates when in vehicles (or use a harness), and most dogs must ride in a crate if they fly by plane. Choose a crate that is large enough for your dog to stand up and turn around but not so large that she will be tossed around in case of a car accident. Dogs can be injured in crates if the crate is too large. For more information about choosing the perfect crate, see Chapter 5: How You Can Enjoy Safe and Hassle-Free Trips With Your Puppy.

3. Make sure that you have toys for your puppy before you bring her home. Your puppy will be coming into a place that is strange to her and she will appreciate something fun to cheer her up. Choose a few things from different toy categories such as balls, ropes, squeakies, stuffed animal-type toys, and so on. Your puppy will soon let you know what kind of toy she likes best. Toys can also be used as rewards during training.

Treats make great rewards for good behavior during training. Treats should be very small and soft. If you are using commercial treats, then break them into smaller pieces. Natural alternatives are chopped vegetables (no onion or garlic – they are poisonous to dogs – see Chapter 2: Nutritious Food for a Well-Fed and Healthy Dog), cooked meat and unsalted popcorn.

Puppy's First Training Lessons

There is nothing quite as sweet, cute, fun, exciting – or as naughty – as a puppy. You can expect to have tons of love and happiness all jammed into your puppy's first year. But in addition to the love you give your puppy, you will also need to provide some gentle training to make sure she grows up to be a well-adjusted, healthy, happy adult dog and not a spoiled brat. There are some basics that every puppy needs to learn. You can start training your puppy as young as eight to 10 weeks of age.

As a bonus I have created 3 online puppy classes for you! The three classes cover:

- How to Raise a Confident Puppy
- How to Raise a Healthy Puppy
- How to Raise an Obedient Puppy

Register here for access to these classes.

Potty training

When you bring your new puppy home the first thing you will want to start is puppy's potty routine. How to teach your puppy to eliminate outside or in a designated area is explained in Chapter 9: The Sure-Fire Way to Get Your Puppy Potty Trained In a Week.

Confidence building

Building confidence in your puppy is about allowing her to become accustomed to your lifestyle. This is so she won't be afraid of new things.

Humans lead busy, interactive and noisy lives. We are exposed to a lot of things, situations and people that would be quite foreign to a dog. As such, socializing your puppy with different people, places, things, noises and activities is a key aspect of confidence building. The window of opportunity for ensuring your puppy is well-socialized is between one and five months. During this short period of time it's your job to provide a stimulating and varied environment – you can do this by:

- Ensuring that your puppy grows to like people generally. Take your puppy out to meet your friends and family. And let visitors pat her.
- Ensuring that your puppy grows to like dogs generally. Let her meet other friendly dogs on a leash where dogs are welcome (such as parks, pet supply stores) as soon as her vaccinations are complete (you can check what a typical vaccination schedule will involve in Chapter 8: Things You Can Do to Help Your Precious Pup Live a Long and Healthy Life). Make sure you ask the other dogs' owners' permission prior to approach.
- Encouraging strangers to pet your puppy. Take treats with you and give them to strangers so they can pat your puppy and give her treats. (This won't make your dog any less welcoming of suspicious people. A secure dog knows the difference between friend and foe).
- Enrolling in a puppy preschool, puppy party or puppy kindergarten. Here your puppy will meet other puppies her age. She will be able to play, meet other friendly owners, and learn some basic good manners in class. These classes are highly recommended. They are usually offered by kennel clubs, animal shelters, pet stores and dog trainers.
- Ensuring that your dog becomes accustomed to different types of noises at different volumes. Sound desensitization is the process of helping your puppy get used to some of the many loud and strange noises that she will encounter in life. Many dogs are afraid of loud noises such as fireworks, thunderstorms and sounds they haven't heard before. By using sound desensitization you can

gently teach her to accept strange noises and to understand that there is nothing frightening about them. In the next section, I'll show you how to desensitize your puppy to strange sounds.

The more confidence you can instill in your puppy, the more confident she will be as an adult. Confident puppies are less likely to develop separation anxiety and other behavioral problems later in life.

Sounds of a lifetime

I have developed an MP3 with everyday sounds so new puppy owners can teach their puppies how to remain relaxed around household sounds. Register at http://yourdogneedsyou.com/puppy-bonus/ and I'll send you a link to my MP3 with the following sound bites:

- Lawnmowers and leaf blowers
- Babies and children
- Phones
- Traffic: cars, trams, dirt bikes and trucks
- Thunderstorms
- Music
- Gun shots and artillery
- Door bells
- Vacuum cleaner
- Hair dryer
- Aeroplanes
- Fireworks

As you can see, these are all sounds that your puppy may encounter. By using recordings you can control when your puppy encounters these sounds and how loud the noise will be. You can be there with her when she hears these noises. You can encourage her to be confident by being cheerful and relaxed when these recordings are played. You may wish to give your puppy treats as she listens, so she understands that nothing bad will happen.

One way to use these recordings is like this: play one of the sounds for your puppy and if she reacts calmly you can praise her and give her a treat. If she is scared, stay calm and cheerful, and play the sound again at a lower volume. Encourage the puppy to play and ignore the sound. When she plays and ignores the sound, praise her and give her a treat. It's that simple. You can use some of the puppy's favorite toys while the sound plays to encourage her to play. Make the sounds fun for your puppy.

You could gather each of these items together, such as a vacuum cleaner, a hair dryer, fireworks, and so on, and teach your puppy about the sounds individually, but it is much easier to teach your puppy about the sounds when you use recordings of the noises. Then your puppy can identify the sounds – and know that they are okay – when she encounters them in real life. Playing these sounds at the time and place of your choosing, when you can be positive and encouraging for your puppy, can do wonders to desensitize your puppy to these and other loud or unexpected sounds.

Sound desensitization is very effective for puppies and helps them develop into confident dogs that are not afraid of hearing these sounds in real life.

Independence training

Raising an independent dog means your dog will remain calm and secure, even when she doesn't have access to you at all times. A dog that frets or experiences anxiety in your absence can engage in problem behaviors such as excessive barking, shadowing (this is when your dog follows you around constantly), destruction, hyperactivity and regression in potty training.

Here are seven keys to raising an independent dog:

1. Do not acknowledge your dog as you return to your house. If you make a fuss, your dog will fret in your absence and long for that special attention she expects upon your return. It's best to ignore

your puppy for about 10 minutes after your arrival, later you can calmly acknowledge her.

2. Give your dog an occupation as you leave the house. In this way, your puppy sees your departure as a positive event. More information on how you can occupy your dog when she's home alone can be found in Chapter 4: Games To Keep Your Puppy Happy and Allow You Both to Bond Beautifully.

3. If you have several people in your home, see that each family member shares responsibility for the puppy's welfare. This means that activities such as feeding, walking, play, potty and training should be done by different people in the household. In this way, your puppy won't come to rely solely on one person for her survival and therefore won't regard one particular person as her 'savior'.

4. Ignore your puppy's demands for attention (via poking, pawing or whining).

5. Make your puppy 'work' for your attention and affection. This can be as simple as doing a quick training exercise, then rewarding with play afterwards. Your dog will learn that you do not give away 'freebies' and that she must behave to be acknowledged.

6. Your puppy should not have constant access to you. This means that even when you are home there will be times when your puppy should not be able to reach you. This can be as simple as ensuring that your dog is in an x-pen or in the yard while you are home. Or you can even use a baby gate to section off part of the house. For puppies, initial periods of separation should be very short (a matter of minutes). These periods of separation can then be lengthened gradually.

7. Give your puppy her own haven. A special, enclosed space such as a crate can be your puppy's 'home'. This is where your puppy can sleep, play or relax without interference from any family. This space gives your puppy a place to feel safe and secure. Never send your dog to this place as a punishment (otherwise it will no longer have a positive association). Also, never drag your dog out of this space or allow children to poke or annoy the dog while she's in there. Later, I'll show you how to crate train your puppy.

Crate training

If you have a puppy then you have already discovered that puppies can be: (i) naughty at times; (ii) destructive and messy in the house; and (iii) sleepy, especially after they use up their energy playing. Crate training is a good solution for some of your puppy's less desirable behaviors, such as chewing and house soiling. It will also keep her out of trouble when you can't be home. A crate also provides your puppy with a safe place to sleep and rest.

What type of crate should you choose?

Purchase a crate that will be large enough for your puppy when she's an adult. Most manufacturers give good guidance regarding which crate is right for which breed (or mix) so check the labels or tags. When in doubt, get a crate that is a little larger rather than one that's too small. However, don't get an enormous crate that will be too big for your dog when she's full-grown. Dogs generally like to feel well-insulated and comforted in their crates, like a den. They won't feel safe in a huge space.

If you choose an adult-sized crate for your puppy, then fill the extra space with blankets – this way the dog will not soil the crate as they do not like to pee or poop in their living space. If the crate is too big, the puppy may use the crate as a potty, which is exactly the behavior you are trying to discourage!

There are several different kinds of crates: hard plastic airline crates, wire crates, and canvas crates. There are even wicker crates and other unusual crates. They are all fine for different purposes. Canvas, wicker and other crates are usually not a good choice for a puppy, however, since they are easily torn or chewed. Choose a hard plastic or wire crate for crate training.

Your puppy's first reaction to the crate

It's not hard to crate train a puppy but your puppy may complain about it at first, depending on her early experiences with a crate. Some breeders use a crate as part of their whelping set-up so some puppies are used to them from birth. They have no objection to spending time in a crate or sleeping in one. To them a crate is a cozy, safe place that they associate with their mother and littermates.

Other puppies, however, may not have seen a crate before. Initially, at least, they may think of being in the crate as jail time. Since you may not know whether your puppy has any experience with a crate it's always a good idea to introduce the crate slowly.

Three steps to easy crate training

1. Allow your puppy to explore the crate.

    Once you have the right crate you should place it in a spot in your home where your puppy can explore it. Leave the door wide open. Place a comfortable sheepskin mat or some towels in the crate and put some treats and toys inside. Many puppies will go inside to get the treats. Your puppy may decide to take a nap there. That's fine - you should let her sleep there with the door open. Let her get used to going in and out of the crate as she likes. You can also begin feeding your puppy dinner in the crate, with the door open.

2. Introduce short periods of crate time.

    After your puppy has become used to the crate you can start closing the door for short periods of time while you are home with your puppy. Close the door for a couple of minutes and give your puppy something good to chew on while she's in the crate. Some puppies may not notice that you have closed the door. They will be focused on the chewy. Other puppies may protest the closed door. It is best to open the door after a couple of minutes and let your puppy out when the puppy is quiet. Do this a few times each day for several days. You can gradually keep your puppy in the crate for longer periods of time, always making sure that you are home with her.

Your puppy should begin to get used to spending some time in the crate. Make sure you always give her something safe to occupy her while she's in there. You should not expect her to spend long periods of time in the crate at this stage, especially if she's very young, as she may soil her space or become distressed.

Eventually you can practice going outside for a few minutes while your puppy is in the crate. Your puppy may howl but you will need to ignore it. Then, once settled, you can go back inside and let her out. The key is not to make a fuss when you let your puppy out. In this way she will not become too excited when you return. Your puppy will learn that you will always come back and so she will not fret while you are away.

3. Gradually increase crate time.

    You can gradually be gone for longer periods. If your puppy whines, howls or freaks out, then cut the time she is left in the crate by half and slowly build up the length of your absences as your puppy remains calm in her crate. When your puppy is still quite young, remember that she will need to be toileted frequently so ensure she is let out often. If she soils her crate this may lead to a bad habit that is hard to break.

Outcome - a happy crate trained puppy!

If you follow these suggestions your puppy will be crate trained in just a few weeks. Some puppies learn faster than others. Some puppies will calm down and take a nap when you leave while others may bark and object at first. The keys are to ensure: (i) your puppy knows that you will return; (ii) the crate is a pleasant place (never scold or punish her while she's in her crate); and (iii) you do not make a big fuss when you leave and return.

Training Your Dog to Be a Good K9 Citizen

The goal of training is not only about moulding your puppy into a confident and secure pet, but also giving your puppy clear guidelines for what is acceptable and unacceptable behavior. If your puppy knows her 'good manners', then she will turn out to be a loyal, fun and easy-going pet. The following is a set of commands that you can teach your puppy so she knows how to obey your instructions.

Teach your dog to "stand"

Standing is a great position to teach your dog; it is particularly useful when you need your dog to stand for a veterinary check up. You can teach your dog to stand using your hands to guide the dog into position with these five simple steps:

1. Kneel beside your dog, with your dog's head at your left and her rump to your right.
2. Hook two of your left fingers under your dog's collar so they are pointing towards your dog's tail.
3. Prop up your dog with your right hand by placing it under the dog's chest area (by hugging your dog from above). As you perform this step, say "stand".
4. Keep the dog in this position for three to four seconds, release and reward your dog.
5. Slowly increase the length of the stand (with your hands still in place) and eventually you will be able to allow your dog stand without being guided.

Here are some quick fixes to common problems associated with training your dog to stand:

- *"My dog sits as I try to position her correctly"*: Make sure you firmly hold the dog's rib cage up with your right hand and do not allow the dog to sit.
- *"My dog seems uncomfortable and cagey"*: Make sure your right hand is under the dog's rib cage and not under her abdomen. Applying pressure to your dog's abdomen can cause discomfort.
- *"My dog squirms or won't stay still"*: Make sure you firmly hold the dog in place. If you 'give in' when the dog struggles against you, she will learn to get her way by wrestling you.

Teach your dog to "sit"

The sit command is one of the first commands to be taught as part of obedience training. People assume that the sit and stay commands should be taught separately when, in fact, you can teach your dog to "stay sitting".

In this way, when you teach your dog to sit, she will eventually learn to remain in the sit position until released or commanded to do another task. This means you do not ever have to say "stay" to your dog.

This command can be used to maintain control of your dog and ensures that she understands you are the boss. For example, you can use the sit command to stop your dog from rushing through doorways ahead of you; as pack leader you should always walk ahead of your dog. This is also a great command to teach before every mealtime. This way, your dog learns to sit and wait for her meal.

There are two ways you can teach your dog to sit. I'll explain both ways and you can choose which method is best for you and your dog.

Using the treat as a 'lure'

1. You and your dog should be standing and facing one another. Take a step away from your dog to encourage her to stand if she's sitting.

2. Have a treat ready in your right hand and hold your dog's lead in your left hand.
3. Allow your dog to see that you have a treat in your hand.
4. In a sweeping motion, move the treat from under your dog's chin to just above dog's nose (between the dog's eyes).
5. Slowly and gently move the treat towards the dog's eyes so that the dog needs to tilt her head backwards. This compels the dog backwards into a sitting position.

6. Just before your dog sits, say "sit" and give her the treat. Your dog may immediately stand again – this is fine as she is learning a new skill.

7. Once your dog is routinely sitting, introduce your release word so you can turn sit into stay (see Ground Rule 20 above). You won't have to say "stay", rather the goal is ensure that your dog will sit until you release her. Initially, releases should be given almost immediately. Then gradually increase the time, initially for a few seconds and slowly to longer and longer periods.

8. Once your dog sits for longer periods (between 30 seconds to two minutes), you can start putting some distance between you and your dog. After directing your dog to sit, take a step away from your dog. Then return to your dog and release her. Slowly and gradually increase the amount of steps you take away from your dog. If you take too many steps too quickly, your dog may move before you release her – so take a gradual and patient approach.

Another way to teach "sit"

If the lure is not working for you and your dog, you can try a different approach. This method is very effective as you are using your hands to carefully maneuver the dog into a sit position.

1. Kneel with your dog in front of you. Your dog's head should be to your right and your dog's rump to your left.
2. Hook the index and middle fingers of your right hand under your dog's collar at the back of the dog's neck, so that your palm is facing up.

3. Say "sit".
4. Firmly and gently tuck your dog's rump in towards the ground. If your dog resists, slightly rock her rump sideways as this will destabilize her hind legs and compel her to sit.

Do not push down on your dog's spine – this may cause serious injury!

5. As you are tucking your dog's rump in, you can also very lightly tug up on your dog's collar with your right hand.
6. Hold your dog in that position for a few seconds, release and reward your dog with praise and/or a treat.
7. Eventually, you'll notice that you do not need to maneuver your dog into a sit position.

You can now start putting some distance between you and your dog. After directing your dog to sit, stand up, then release and reward her. Slowly and gradually increase the distance between you and your dog. Always return to release and reward your dog.

Teach your dog to "drop"

Teaching your dog to drop is very important. It is a great way to keep control of your dog and ensure that she remains calm and relaxed if left in a stay position for longer periods.

Here is how you can teach your dog to 'drop':

1. Kneel beside your sitting dog, with the dog's head to your right. (Your dog should know the sit command before learning "drop").
2. Place your left hand on your dog's rump. Do not push your dog's spine; just keep your dog's rump tucked into the ground.

3. Place a treat in front of your dog's nose so that she sees the treat in your right hand. In a slow sweeping motion, lower it to the floor so that the treat is about 6-12 inches (15 - 30 centimetres) from your dog's feet. Hold the treat still. Do not move the treat closer then farther away from your dog's nose, as your dog will find this 'game of tag' tiresome and unrewarding.

4. Just as your dog lies flat on the floor, say "drop" and give her the treat.

Timing is key – say "drop" only as your dog reaches the floor. In this way, your dog will learn to associate the word "drop" with the actual action of lying on the floor. Initially, your dog may immediately stand again – this is fine as she is learning a new skill.

5. If your dog does not move towards the treat, use an item your dog really wants, a tastier morsel food or a beloved toy. Sometimes patience is needed, but your dog will eventually understand what she needs to do.

Never try and push your dog down as she will automatically resist.

6. Once your dog is routinely dropping, introduce your release word so you can turn drop into stay (see Ground Rule 20 above). You won't have to say "stay", rather the goal is ensure that your dog will stay in the drop position until you release her. Initially, releases should be given almost immediately. Gradually increase the time, initially for a few seconds and slowly to longer periods.

Teach your dog to "come"

The recall command, like sit and stay, forms the basis of good obedience training. A dog that comes when called is more easily controlled and less vulnerable to hazards such as roadways.

Here is the recall training in six steps:

1. Make sure your dog is on a lead and is not looking at you.

2. When your dog is looking away from you, say her name. Praise her when she looks at you.

3. Open your arms wide or lift one arm in the air, say "come!" in an excited tone and take a few steps backwards.

4. As your dog approaches you, gently capture her. Release and reward.
5. Using a longer lead, slowly increase distance between you and your dog.

Eventually, you can try this training without having the dog on a lead. Make sure you are in a safe, confined space when you do this (in case your intrepid dog tries to run off!)

Some extra tips to get good recalls

Here are some things you can do to make your recall training even more effective:

Play little games with your puppy where you reward her with treats and affection for giving you attention when you say her name.

Never, ever call your dog over to punish her or to do something unpleasant (such as a bath or trimming nails). If you do, she will be reluctant to come when called as she might not know whether you are calling her for good or bad reasons. Your puppy must know that whenever she is called to you, it's only for good reasons.

You can crouch down during recall to make yourself more appealing to your dog.

Before recalling your dog, make sure she sees that you have a toy or treat in your hand. This will entice your dog to come more quickly. If your puppy has an older canine playmate, you can use that dog as a lure by keeping that dog next to you as you recall your puppy.

Play tag where you are always the one being chased. This way, your dog will come to love 'catching' you. This strategy can be used to great advantage during recall training.

Troubleshooting the recall

Here are some quick fixes to common problems associated with recall training:

- *"My dog refuses to come"*: If your dog does not respond to your recall, then you can behave excitedly and make high pitched sounds like "pup, pup, puppy!". You can also gently tug the lead.
- *"My dog runs to me before I say come"*: Praise your dog anyway. Never, ever punish her for coming to you.
- *"My dog won't come unless I have a treat in my hand"*: Play tag, crouch or lie down to entice your dog to come.
- *"My dog seems to veer off in another direction as she nears me"*: Simply continue jogging backwards and wave a reward such as a toy or food treat in front of you.
- *"My dog ignores me when I say her name"*: Train your dog to look at you when you say her name. See the next section on how to do this.

Teach your dog her name

It's important that your puppy learns to give you attention when you command her to do so - this means she must look at you when you call her name. Follow these steps to train your puppy to learn her name:

1. Wave a small treat in front of your dog's face so that your dog starts to follow the treat with her eyes.

2. Bring the treat up to your nose - your dog's eyes should follow the treat so that she is looking at you in the face.

3. Say the dog's name, praise and give the treat.

You can do this five to six times a day. Your dog will quickly get into the habit of looking at your face when you say her name.

Teach your dog leash manners

Before teaching your puppy leash manners, you must ensure that you have correctly fitted a collar. A collar that is too loose is a dangerous hazard as it may come off when your dog is near a busy road. A collar that is too tight may constrict your dog's breathing.

A collar is a proper fit when you are able to slide only one or two fingers comfortably through the collar when your dog is wearing it.

You can measure your dog's neck with a soft measuring tape, and then adjust the collar to match. Even if you do this, it is likely that the collar will need adjustment once it is on her. However, measuring beforehand means that you will need to only have minimal adjustments once the collar is on the dog.

Make sure your dog's collar has a tag with your contact details clearly etched into it.

Getting used to the collar and leash

Your puppy may not like the collar at first and may create a fuss. So, put the collar on for short stints to begin with. Gradually increase the length of time, making sure your dog is distracted with treats and play. It's normal for a dog to whine or fuss so leave the collar on until the dog has settled. If you immediately remove the collar when the dog fusses or whines, then your dog will learn to get her way by whining.

Once your puppy is used to a collar, you can begin getting your puppy used to a lead.

Allow your dog to sniff and familiarize herself with the lead. However, do not use it as a toy as this will encourage your dog to bite and play with the lead when you take her for walks.

First hook the collar to the lead and allow the lead to hang freely on the ground. Allow your dog to explore her surroundings with the lead attached (but not held on to).

You can, if you want, drape the lead over the dog's back and play with your dog.

Once your puppy is comfortable with the fact that there is a lead attached, you can pick up the lead. Don't lead her around yet – instead let her lead you to wherever she's going. This first session should be short and fun. You can make subsequent sessions incrementally longer and let her explore the yard and house as she chooses. This allows the dog to associate freedom of movement with the collar and lead.

If and when your dog strains on the lead, stop and encourage your puppy to return to you. Making light-hearted sounds like "pup pup puppy!" There is never a need to yank or jerk the lead or pull your dog back to you.

Make this whole process as pleasant as possible; this means you should praise and play with your dog and give her treats or meals while the lead is attached.

Teaching your puppy to "heel"

After your puppy or dog is comfortable with the lead and you have done some initial lead training, you can begin to teach your puppy to heel. Until your dog learns to heel, all walks should be treated as a training session – so keep walks short and fun.

Begin the walk with the dog to your left. Start off and say "heel". Walk briskly, but be mindful of your dog's pace. For example, toy breeds and smaller dogs require a slower pace.

If your puppy pulls ahead, you can try these two techniques:

- Stop walking. Never ever keep walking when your puppy is pulling on the lead, this only rewards her behavior and reinforces the habit. Do not proceed ahead until the dog is at your side again. You might have to coax your dog back to you.

- Simply turn and walk in the opposite direction. In this way, your dog learns that if she pulls, she won't get any further.

  You can make walking fun by walking in zigzags and by giving her rewards. This will serve to stimulate your puppy and encourage her to follow you. This is important because when you're both out on a walk you're basically competing for your puppy's attention with all the other wonderful sights and smells. So make yourself exciting and fun.

At curbs you can have your puppy sit beside you, and as you move off again say "heel".

Teach your dog to calmly greet people

Dogs often lick each other on the face or nether regions as part of their greeting rituals. It is therefore natural for dogs to jump up on people upon meeting them, hoping to engage them in a friendly way. However, this is an unacceptable habit, and it is your responsibility as a dog owner to ensure that you teach your dog to greet people calmly, whether these people are visitors to your home or passers-by in public areas.

Here are some effective tips to deter or prevent jumping:

- Do not pick up a dog in response to jumping as this is seen as a reward and will only encourage this unwanted behavior.

- As your dog jumps on you, fold your arms, avoid eye contact and swiftly turn away.

- If your dog's jumping is ingrained, then try this: As your dog jumps on you, slightly lift your knee so that it connects with a soft bump to her chest. (Do not allow others to try this on your dog, as a miscalculation could result in a nasty kick).

- You can also try holding your dog's paws as she jumps on you. A light squeeze to the paws is generally unpleasant to dogs.

- Do not tolerate hyperactivity and attention-seeking from your dog when you have guests in your home. This means no jumping, barking or whining when people arrive. Have visitors ignore the dog when they come so the dog does not get over-stimulated. If the dog jumps on people, take the dog away until she's calm. Bring the dog back to where the visitors are and allow the dog to remain while calm. Consistently remove the dog from the room whenever she misbehaves. In order to have control over the dog when visitors arrive, have the dog on a lead. Always have a mat, crate or other resting place in your living room so the dog can have a place to settle when people are visiting. Visitors should wait until the dog is calm before gently praising and patting the dog.

Three ways to stop your dog jumping on you

Gently Squeeze paws

Knee nudge

Turn away & ignore

How to stop your puppy from chewing on things

If you've ever come home to find your favorite shoes chewed into pieces or found the remote control after your puppy has chomped on it, then you probably already know that dogs like to chew. But you may not know that there can actually be a number of reasons for a dog's chewing behavior. Here's a look at some reasons why dogs chew and how you can manage this issue.

1. Like human babies, puppies are born without any teeth. This means that for the first few weeks of life they are cutting teeth and learning to use them. During their first few weeks they will have very sharp little 'milk teeth'. Between four and seven months they will be getting their adult teeth. All of this tooth business means that your puppy will be cutting a lot of teeth and looking for things to chew on! She may chew on you, soft things, hard things and anything she can find to put in her mouth. Nothing at all is safe during this time. If you leave it lying around your puppy will chew on it.

    You can help your puppy a lot by giving her lots of things of her own to chew on. Make sure you provide a good variety of chewies – give her things with different textures such as soft toys, hard chews, hard rubber Kongs, indestructible chew toys. You can even wring out a wet wash cloth and freeze it for your puppy. Your puppy will probably like the hard cold texture of the cloth to chew on and it's easy to wet it and re-freeze it again later for her. The more things of her own that your puppy has to chew on, the less likely your puppy will be to chew on your things.

2. Loneliness and boredom. Dogs that are left alone all day with nothing to do often act out and get into trouble by chewing on things. They can become very destructive. A bored dog will find things to chew on. You can help keep your dog occupied by providing her with plenty of her own things to chew on. Give her toys to snuggle with, hard things to chew on, balls to chase and some good interactive toys that she has to figure out in order to get treats.

   If your dog is lonely and bored you may also wish to leave the TV or radio on for her. Have a neighbor or friend drop by during the day to see your dog. Perhaps have a dog walker take her for a walk during the day. And, it always helps if you can spend more time with your dog yourself. Make the time you have with your dog count. It will also help if you increase your dog's exercise when you're home. Dogs that get plenty of exercise are more likely to spend their daytime hours resting and less likely to spend their time alone being destructive.

3. Separation anxiety. Your dog may chew on your belongings when you're gone. This can be a sign of loneliness, boredom or separation anxiety. A dog with separation anxiety will also have problems when you leave her alone in a room while you're still in the house. She won't want to allow you out of her sight at all. If you suspect that your dog does have separation anxiety you should talk to your veterinarian about possible behavior modification approaches and medication for your dog.

4. Normal chewing. Keep in mind that some chewing is perfectly normal for your dog. Not all chewing is bad. For your dog,

chewing can be very soothing and relaxing since it satisfies a natural instinct to gnaw and chew on things. It's a good idea to provide your dog with a regular source of safe chew toys so she can satisfy this instinct. Always remember that the more toys and chewies of her own that your dog has, the less likely she is to chew on your things.

Reduce your puppy's mouthing and nipping

For puppies, biting is a natural behavior that may subside by the time they are four months old. However, it is not guaranteed this problem will disappear on its own, so it is recommended that biting is discouraged from the start. Many owners view this behavior as playful, but the puppy may also be testing what you will tolerate.

What are the best ways to stop a snappy puppy? Just do what other dogs would do! Puppies first learn from their mother or litter mates that biting is inappropriate. When a puppy bites, the other dog may respond by giving a short sharp 'yelp!', withdrawing, growling or biting back. We all know that biting back is not the way to go! But there is plenty of merit in the other strategies. Let's look at what you can do when your puppy bites you:

- The short sharp yelp: A short, high pitched 'ouch!' or 'yelp!' will startle the dog into ceasing the biting. Make sure the yelp is high pitched but not too loud – the aim is to startle, not frighten, the puppy. All dogs instinctively recognize this sound as meaning it has caused pain and it will immediately stop.
- The growl or correction: A verbal correction such as 'no!' or a low guttural growl will give your puppy a clear message that biting is not tolerated.
- Withdrawing: Simply stop and withdraw the part of you that has been bitten. A concurrent growl or yelp will help reinforce the message.

There are also some other things you can do to prevent your puppy growing into a snappy dog. They are:

- Reinforce safe play - when puppy plays nicely, reward her with affection and treats.
- Correct your puppy without using your hands - some dogs grow up having had bad experiences with human hands because they were smacked as a puppy; they may bite hands as a way of protecting themselves. It is therefore important that when you are raising your puppy that you never smack her, otherwise she may grow up to be a 'fear biter'. Use verbal corrections as discussed earlier.

How to Choose a Good Dog Trainer

This guide serves as a way to empower you as a dog owner to train your dog well, however, you might decide to engage the services of a professional dog trainer to help you out. But there are so many dog trainers. How do you know which one to choose? Here are some things to look for in a great dog trainer.

1. Observe. After you have found several possible trainers you should ask if you can observe them working with dogs. See if you can sit in on their classes if they offer group training. How do they interact with other owners and their dogs? Are they brusque? Understanding? Are they rough with dogs? Do they explain things to the owners? Do they repeat things until the dogs are bored or do they keep the dogs interested and happy? It's important to observe a trainer because this gives a good indication of what your training with your dog would be like.
2. Talk to the trainer about their qualifications. Some trainers are certified by professional organizations for dog or animal trainers although not all are. At the very least you should find out about their training specialties. Is most of her or her experience in training dogs for agility or some other sport? This doesn't mean that the trainer can't teach you and your dog the basics

of obedience but it does mean they may have less experience working with some kinds of dogs than others. Ask the trainer about their experience with dogs like yours.

3. Talk to the trainer about her or her training methods. There are a number of different approaches to dog training. These include positive reinforcement such as using a clicker and treats; traditional dog training which uses a slip chain collar; and combination methods. Ask your trainer what methods he or she uses. Some dogs respond better to one method than another or you may have your own preference. It's best to know how the trainer trains before you sign up to work with her.

4. Do ask about price. However, remember that a trainer's rates should not be the sole determination in choosing a trainer. For example, many pet stores offer training classes. They are usually relatively inexpensive for a few weeks of training. However, you can often find a better, more experienced trainer if you are willing to go to another training center and pay a little more. If you are working one-on-one with a trainer or if a trainer is coming to your home to work with you and your dog, you can expect to pay more. However, you and your dog may progress faster because of the focused attention so you may not need as many lessons. If you have a good trainer, you and your dog may learn more, too. So, try to consider the quality of instruction as well as the price when you are choosing a trainer.

5. Intangibles. There are also some intangibles to consider when choosing a dog trainer. Sometimes you just seem to 'click' with someone. Or your dog may really like a particular trainer. Although you may not be able to give a rational reason for these reactions, you should still respect them. These reactions are important.

6. Read their testimonials. Most dog trainers have a website. Make sure you check it out and see what others owners had to say about the dog trainer. A good dog trainer will have many testimonials from different owners. The testimonials will also give you an idea of which dogs the trainer has worked with and what problems

the dog trainer is good at solving. Testimonials are particularly useful if you have not been able to observe the trainer with other dogs.

In summary, when choosing a dog trainer for you and your dog, give consideration to the person's qualifications, training methods, rates and your own reaction to them. And remember to make time to observe them at work with other dogs and owners. If you follow these suggestions then you should be able to choose a great trainer for you and your dog.

Chapter 8: Things You Can Do to Help Your Precious Pup Live a Long and Healthy Life

As an owner it's your responsibility to give your puppy the best start in life and to support her health throughout her adult and senior years. In this chapter I'll share some tips for ensuring that your dog lives a longer and happier life. When it comes to your dog's health, prevention is always better – and cheaper – than cure. The best health comes from understanding that most of your interaction with your puppy, whether it is via training, grooming or other activities, will have a real impact on your dog's mental and physical health. Therefore, this chapter is best read in conjunction with the following manuals in this series so you can maintain your dog's vitality on a holistic level:

- Information on what foods are good for your dog, and dietary options, can be found in Chapter 2: Nutritious Food for a Well-Fed and Healthy Dog.
- Advice on the best way to care for your dog's general hygiene, wellbeing and dental care can be found in Chapter 3: The Best Ways to Look After Your Precious Puppy's Coat, Eyes, Ears, Teeth and Paws.
- Information on what types of exercise and activities best suit your dog to keep her occupied, active and alert can be found in

Chapter 4: Games To Keep Your Puppy Happy and Allow You Both to Bond Beautifully.

- Guidance on how to develop your dog's confidence and independence and how to ensure she listens to you can be found in Chapter 7: How Can You Train Your Dog to Be Remarkably Obedient and Wonderfully Well-Behaved.

In this chapter, I'll explain:

- The importance and schedules associated with worming, fleas and vaccinations.
- The pros and cons of pet insurance.
- How to develop a good relationship with your vet and what you and your vet should monitor as your puppy grows.

Your puppy's development and general health should be monitored in collaboration with your vet, as these manuals are not meant to be a substitute for veterinary medical advice.

Life Stages

Newborn to weaned puppy

Newborn puppies are deaf, blind and are unable to regulate their own body temperature (hence they keep warm by sleeping bundled against their littermates). However, they are born with a sense of taste, touch and smell. At this stage, puppies toilet only after being stimulated by their mother. At about three weeks, puppies begin to learn to potty away from their sleeping and eating area.

Puppies are completely dependent on their mother for milk until three weeks, at which time they can start to digest soft food. They are completely weaned by six weeks. They grow quickly: their weight doubles in the first week.

From two to four weeks, puppies start to gain their sight and hearing, and puppy teeth emerge. At about three weeks they start investigating their environment and start learning from their mother and littermates.

By five weeks a puppy's eyesight has developed. They recognize people and become more interested in interacting with their littermates and carers. Their mother will begin to discipline them, which is how they learn to respect hierarchy and rules of interaction. For example, a puppy who is not disciplined by her mother or any littermates for biting too hard can grow up to be quite nippy as an adult.

Because puppies learn from their environment at birth, puppies that are handled and talked to are more confident and resilient than their counterparts who are raised in an isolated environment like cages or puppy mills.

Take home age

It is usually between eight and twelve weeks that a puppy is taken home by a new owner. Because a puppy learns from her littermates and mother, a puppy might lack the complete set of skills necessary to interact properly with other dogs if she is taken away earlier than eight weeks of age.

At this age puppies are still learning a lot about their environment; in fact, how a puppy is taught and what she is exposed to at this stage can determine how well a puppy will be socialized to deal with sounds, people, things and their environment.

Puppies will engage in behavior that may seem odd or annoying. This is quite normal and it is important that you don't punish your dog for:

- Chewing and biting – redirect your puppy to chew toys.
- Humping – this behavior is not sexual. Rather it's a way of experimenting with how to interact with others. Discourage your dog from doing this with people.
- Temper tantrums and growling – this is especially true for puppies who have bossy personalities. Be firm, consistent and provide structure, without resorting to punishment.
- Hyperactive episodes – there'll be times when your puppy may rocket around the house like a lunatic. This is normal and is usually followed by a nap or resting time.
- Bursts of play and sleeping – your puppy will play, wrestle, demand attention and then suddenly will want nothing more than some alone time and some sleep.
- Startles and nervousness – between eight and twelve weeks some puppies may become nervous and startle easily. Too much affection and reassurance during these episodes may result in the dog thinking it's okay to be scared. Assuming the object of the fear is benign, don't acknowledge your puppy's fear; instead handle and talk to the object and reward any show of bravery with praise and treats.

Adolescence

A dog's adolescence usually occurs between four and 18 months of age. This period can be difficult; your puppy may be defiant and forgetful of her obedience skills. This is normal and requires patience and revision of lessons.

Sexual maturity

During this period your puppy will become an adolescent and reach sexual maturity. A female dog can have her first estrus (or heat) between five and 10 months old. A heat can last about three weeks, during which she might lose drops of blood or serum (a watery form of blood). You can purchase protective bloomers from a pet store. She might behave nervously or depressed, and might try to run away. If she manages to escape, there is the danger that she might find herself a mate and get pregnant. If you wish to breed your female, many vets recommend that she should not be allowed to become pregnant on the first heat.

A male dog's testicles will descend between two and six months. If they have not at age six months of age, see your vet as health complications may arise. A male dog's testosterone levels will make him responsive to females on heat, as well as possibly challenging other male dogs. Your male dog will go from squatting to cocking his leg to toilet and he will be able to father a litter at age six months.

Speutering your dog

Spaying refers to the removal of the female reproductive system. This includes the ovaries and the uterus. Neutering is the removal of the testicles from the male dog. Speutering is a term used to cover both.

Most dogs are spayed or neutered when they are between five and eight months old. However, it is possible to spay or neuter a dog at as young as two months old without affecting the dog's growth patterns. The risks and benefits of pediatric speutering should be considered in consultation with your vet. Neutering male dogs early on in life often leads to dogs less aggressive than dogs who have not been neutered (or ones that have been neutered later in life). The removal of the testicles inhibits the dog's desire to mark in inappropriate locations, such as in the house.

Neutered dogs don't get distracted by other dogs (especially female dogs) so much which means they pay more attention to training. They tend to be significantly calmer than dogs who have not been fixed. In addition, without sex drive dogs tend to be much more laid back. The neutering process also prevents future health problems in male dogs, in particular prostrate problems and testicular cancer, both fairly common problems in aging, intact males.

Spaying of a female dog is considered a routine surgery and the risk of complication is low. However, your dog will have to go through the healing process for 7-10 days, and will need to be monitored and kept relatively calm during this period.

The benefits of spaying before the first heat include a decrease in breast infections and a measurable and significant decrease in the chance of getting breast cancer. Once spayed your female dog won't have to go into heat anymore. Spaying also prevents false pregnancies as well as 'pyometra' (infection of the uterus). Pyometra is a very serious condition that often results in expensive emergency surgery as it can be difficult detect in its early stages. Symptoms of an infected uterus include increased drinking, depression and even collapse. Pyometra can be fatal, if left untreated.

Maturity

At this time, all your hard work, training and care will begin to pay off. With the trials of adolescence over, you'll now begin to enjoy a sensible, healthy adult dog.

Remember, though, that learning for dogs never stops. Even the best behaved dogs need refreshers on obedience skills. You can even capitalize on your dog's skills and natural abilities by teaching your dog simple tricks like barking on command, rolling over and fetch.

Even though your dog will be less work, she will still have needs: keep her mind and body active so she stays alert, happy and healthy.

Senior dog

Small dogs reach their senior years at about 10 years of age, whilst some larger breeds can be considered senior at five.

As your dog ages you'll being to notice these changes:

- Your dog will spend more time napping and be less energetic.
- Tolerance to exercise may drop, so she may not be able to walk as fast or as far as she once could. It's important to adjust her exercise routine, so your dog does not become overly tired, stressed or injured. Having said that, do not stop exercising your dog altogether as your dog may miss these fun times and also put on weight. Instead, opt for shorter sessions as tolerated. Exercise is a great way to keep your dog's muscles as lean as possible, which may assist otherwise sore or arthritic joints.
- Your dog may become prone to weight gain and need smaller meals.
- The muzzle may become greyer and she may get fatty lumps under her skin or warts around her face. Many lumps are harmless, but have a vet check them just in case.
- Your dog's hearing, eyesight and sense of smell may diminish. That's why when training your dog, it's important to use both verbal and hand signals so when her senses start to fail you can communicate with her in different ways.
- An otherwise housebroken dog may potty inside the house; do not punish her as these are accidental. Talk to your vet about treatment options.
- Your dog might display confusion, aggression or forgetfulness. These behaviors may have underlying physical causes, so have a vet check her out.

Apart from certain dietary changes (see Chapter 2: Nutritious Food for a Well-Fed and Healthy Dog), it's important that you provide your dog with a comfortable place to rest and sleep. Ensure that her bed is soft and caters to arthritic dogs.

Joint pain and arthritis are very common in aging dogs. As a general rule human medications can harm (and can be fatal) to your dog, but supplements made for people such as fish oil and glucosamine can help ease your dog's joint stiffness. Before giving your dog any supplements, talk to your vet about correct doses for your dog's breed and weight.

Signs Your Dog Is Healthy

A healthy dog generally copes with her environment better (that is, experiences less stress and frustration) and has a stronger immune system than her unhealthy counterparts. Checking your puppy for signs of health need not be a formal exercise, you can simply observe your puppy to see that she consistently exhibits the following characteristics:

- Steady development.
- Active and alert (between periods of sleep and rest).
- Flexible, smooth, pale pink to brown or black coat color depending on the breed.
- Glossy coat, which is smooth to touch.
- Healthy weight. For instructions on how to check whether your puppy is at a healthy weight, refer to Chapter 2: Nutritious Food for a Well-Fed & Healthy Dog.
- Well-formed stools: firm and brown in color.
- Bright, clear, shiny, healthy pink area around eyeball (conjunctiva).
- Clean and pink skin inside the ear.
- Short nails.
- Gums are firm, pink, or pigmented with black.
- Clean, sparkling teeth (23 for puppies and 42 for adult dogs).
- No odd lumps in the tissue or indentations of the muscles.
- Urine is clear and yellow.

Signs Your Dog Is Unhealthy

The following are signs that your dog's health is suffering due to an illness, disease or parasite:

- Lethargy.
- Irritability.
- Pale eyes or discharge coming from the eyes.
- Coat and skin will have dandruff, bald spots, excessive oiliness, skin irritation, fleas, ticks or parasites.
- Ticks, redness, swelling, excessive yellow or brownish wax or bad smell from the ear.
- Your dog needs to strain to poop, or her poop is runny, watery, black in color, contains blood or whitish bits that look like rice.
- The dog's paws have dirty objects, or seem red or swelled.
- Foul smelling, thick, bubbly, yellow or green nasal discharge.
- Pale or red, inflamed gums.
- Blood in urine or excessive urination within a short period of time.

The above list is a general guideline on how to spot a problem with your dog's health. If you see any of these signs, consult your vet for an accurate diagnosis and treatment.

Your Dog's Vital Signs

Temperature

If you suspect your dog is unwell, but want to make sure, then you can check your dog's internal temperature. There are two ways in which you can take your dog's temperature, via the ear or the rectum:

	Ear	Ear
Normal Temperature	100.0°F − 103.0°F (37.8°C − 39.4°C)	100.5°F − 102.5°F (38.1°C − 39.4°C)
Equipment	Pet ear thermometer	Digital or mercury oral/rectal thermometer
Instructions	1. Place the thermometer deep into the horizontal ear canal. Insert thermometer for length of time as per manufacturer's recommendations (usually 1-3 seconds). Pet-Temp's ear thermometer will 'beep' to signal that it's okay to remove it from your dog's ear. 2. Remove the thermometer and read the temperature.	1. Enlist the help of another as some dogs don't like this. 2. If using mercury thermometer, use your wrist to flick it until the mercury is below 94°F (34.4°C). 3. Lubricate the thermometer with petroleum jelly or water-based lubricant. 4. Have the other person hold the dog's head and front torso with a tight hug. 5. Lift the tail and insert the thermometer carefully and slowly about 1 inch (2.5 cm) into the rectum. The rectum is located just below the tail's base. 6. Hold the thermometer in place for two minutes for mercury thermometers (or until the digital thermometer beeps).
Action	If your dog has a body temperature less than 99.0°F(37.2°C) or over 104.0°F(40.0°C), contact your vet, pet ambulance or pet hospital immediately. High temperatures could mean an infection or heat-related illness. Low temperatures can denote serious problems such as shock.	

Can you determine your dog's temperature by checking her nose or fold beneath her leg and body?

A cold and moist nose is generally a sign that your dog is healthy and hydrated. However, don't solely rely on this to gauge your dog's health. This is because a warm, dry nose is not necessarily a bad sign. For an accurate assessment of your dog's internal temperature, use a thermometer as described above.

Placing the thermometer in the fold between her leg and torso does not give an accurate reading. The temperature in the fold is typically one to two degrees lower than your dog's actual temperature.

Your dog's heart rate

Puppies have heart rates ranging from 180 to 220 beats per minute. The average heart rate for resting adult dogs is generally lower, between 50 and 130 beats per minute, but this depends on the size of the dog. Typical heart rates for a large breed dog (such as a German Shepherd) are between 60 and 120 beats per minute.

Make sure you check your dog's heart rate when her health appears normal and she is resting, so you have a clear indication of your dog's typical heart rate. This will give you a point of comparison if you're checking your dog's rate because you're concerned for her health or when exercising together.

There are two ways in which you can take your dog's heart rate:

	Chest	**Femoral Pulse**
Instructions	1. Place your hand in your dog's armpit, and lay your other hand flat along her chest. 2. Count her heart beats for 15 seconds, then multiply that number by four	1. The femoral pulse can be felt on the inside of the dog's thigh. 2. Find the femur (long bone of her leg) and gently put your fingers in the groove next to the bone. 3. Count her heart beats for 15 seconds, then multiply that number by four.
Action	You dog's pulse should be steady and regular. A weak or irregular pulse can be a sign of illness, disease or parasite. A heart rate that is considerably above the norm may be a sign that your dog is in distress. In either event, contact your vet, pet ambulance or pet hospital immediately.	

At rest, a dog's respiratory rate can be as low as 20 to 24 breaths per minute. However, when dogs are excited they can pant quickly. Your dog should be breathing without difficulty. If your dog is coughing, wheezing or is using her belly muscles to breath, then she might be in distress or be ill.

Respiratory rate

To measure your dog's respiratory rate all you need to do is count how many times she breathes in 15 seconds and multiplythat number by 4.

Choosing the Right Vet

Choosing the right vet is incredibly important and can have a massive impact on your dog's health and longevity, as well as your wallet. Your vet will be your first point of call whenever your dog encounters any health concerns, so it's important to choose someone you can trust. Here are five tips to choosing the right vet for your puppy:

1. Make sure you find a vet before, or soon after, picking up your new puppy. Call or visit your local vets and have a chat. This way you can make a considered decision.

2. When inspecting different veterinary practices, have a look at their kennel area. This will give you an idea of their level of hygiene and care. The kennel area should be clean and warm. The area should also smell relatively clean, however such areas are difficult to keep fresh!

3. For practices where there is more than one vet in attendance, ask whether your puppy will be assigned to one vet only. Some practices have a 'one-vet-one-pet' policy, whilst others simply make appointments based on which vet is available.

4. Your new vet should make you feel welcome and take your concerns seriously. A good vet will answer your questions and freely share information.

5. Check their prices, but don't base your decision solely on price. The old 'you get what you pay for' adage applies to vets as much as it does to other professional services. On the other hand, choose a vet within your budget because there is no point choosing a vet that you cannot afford.

When comparing prices you should look at these particular procedures:

- Vaccinations: ask for the price of the yearly booster. First vaccinations and 'top ups' are usually all priced differently, so to get a comparable price you must ask for the booster price. Vaccinations are independent of your dog's weight so should be the same across the all breeds and sizes.

- De-sexing: ask for the price of the standard neutering procedure of a 10kg (22lbs) female dog. This way you'll make sure that there's no confusion, and you'll get to compare some real prices for the exact same procedure. Spaying bitches is a relatively 'big' operation, since it requires opening the abdomen. It is therefore a really good procedure to compare prices, because the price will include a general anesthetic, a surgical procedure and follow-up visits.
- X-rays: ask for the price of a standard abdominal x-ray for a 10kg (22lbs) dog. Make sure this includes the price for sedating your dog.

When it comes to prices, pet insurance can help ease the cost of care (depending on what type of cover you have). So, ask your vet for a recommendation for pet insurance as well as researching alternatives. Later in this chapter, I'll explain how pet insurance works.

Helping your puppy get familiar with the vet

As adults, we have a tendency to become frightened in uncertain situations. The same is true for puppies. A puppy which is normally confident and calm-tempered at home may become panicky, aggressive, shy or cautious at the vet's surgery. The strange sounds, unusual walking surfaces, new smells and sights might alarm her. Fortunately, there are a few ways you can help your puppy familiarize herself with your vet.

The first steps involve preparation. If your puppy is normally inside and only taken out to relieve herself or for occasional walks, socialize her with new people and places. Taking her out in public around new people and in new environments will not only help her when you take her to the doctor, but might also make her a calmer puppy inside your home. Different places will allow her to see new people of all ages, different clothing styles, and various smells. Try to vary the walking surfaces between tiles, gravel, and dirt or asphalt so that she will not feel as unsure in the vet's office. Try exposing your puppy to new sounds, whether it is vehicles passing by, children playing or umbrellas opening. Exercise patience, though, because your puppy may act up the first few times you change her environment.

You need to make sure that your puppy obeys and responds to you. Educate yourself about obedience training, teach her to lie down, stand up, stay, and sit on your command. If your puppy trusts you to set boundaries and will follow your guidelines, making her feel safer. In addition to training, your puppy should also be comfortable with the way a vet will handle her. Several times a day, pick your puppy up and put her on a countertop so that she will not be afraid of the height of the examination table. Touch all of her body parts as if you are massaging her. Make sure you examine her face, body, legs, and paws, inside her mouth and ears and tail. Squeeze her shoulders and hips gently and lightly press on her spine. Get her acclimated to having various body parts touched. In addition, your vet will give her a bear hug from the front and behind, as well as a belly rub, the position for x-rays, so try these positions, too. Do not forget to reward her with treats!

Before your vet appointment, drive there, sit in the parking lot a few times and give your puppy treats. Ask the receptionist to make a big deal over your puppy and reward her with treats. It is usually best to make the appointment when the doctor is least busy and arrive early so you and your puppy are not frazzled and whisked away. You can ask the staff to give your puppy treats and either ask them for a towel or bring one yourself for your puppy to lie on.

Your puppy may be more comfortable on the floor, so ask your vet if the examination can be performed there instead of the examination table. Remember to give your puppy treats throughout the appointment.

If your puppy is still having difficulty going to the vet's office, ask if you can go immediately from the car into the room, bypassing the reception area altogether. You might also consider giving your puppy calming herbal remedies or arrange for a home visit from the vet (if this option is available).

Pet Insurance

Although pet insurance has been available in the United States since 1982, it's estimated that only 1-2% of pet owners actually have insurance for their pets. Pet insurance is slightly more popular in Canada (an estimated 9% of Canadians have pet insurance) and some 20% of Europeans have pet insurance. Only about 2% of Australian pets are insured.

Why have pet insurance?

Whilst some vet procedures are inexpensive, there are many procedures that can cost thousands of dollars, such as emergency care resulting from tick paralysis or being hit by a car. Surgeries on the knee, leg, heart, spine and brain can each cost thousands of dollars. If you think you cannot afford these expenses and therefore would be faced with choosing between money and your dog's life, then pet insurance is a way to avoid this. Pet insurance is ideal for those wanting to save money on surgeries, procedures and preventative treatments (such as heartworm and ticks) as well as ensuring their dog gets the best possible care.

Pet insurance is most worth considering for the following types of owners:

- People who have a high maintenance pure-breed dog such as a Basset Hound, Boxer, Dalmatian, Great Dane, Keeshond, Newfoundland, Pug, Samoyed or Weimeraner.
- People who own a larger breed of dog. Vet bills for big animals tend to be more expensive than for small dogs.
- Dogs that are accident prone or sensitive.
- Owners who frequently leave their pets in kennels or who vacation with their dogs.
- People on a limited budget.

Types of pet insurance

Pet insurance varies a great deal so, if you are considering purchasing pet insurance, consider what kind of insurance you would like to have.

Your premium will depend on the kind of insurance you choose. Most pet insurance does not cover well-pet visits, such as vaccinations and a yearly physical. If you do choose this kind of coverage, you can expect to pay a very high monthly premium.

Many plans cover accidents and illnesses up to a cut-off point which will vary, depending on the company. However, existing conditions and hereditary illnesses are almost never covered. Some plans do cover cancer treatments.

Deductibles will also vary a great deal, depending on the plan you choose.

Some plans do offer coverage for spaying and neutering, dental procedures and other needs, above and beyond ordinary veterinary visits. You will pay substantially more for these plans in monthly premiums.

Types of plans

There are many options for pet insurers and many of them offer different policy levels, so you will need to read the policies carefully in order to choose which one best fits your dog's needs.

In most cases you can get either a basic plan or a premium plan from an insurer. As you might imagine, the difference is usually what is covered by the plan. Most basic plans will cover accidents and injuries. If you want a plan that covers more, you will have to get a premium plan and pay a premium rate.

In all cases, pet insurance is based on the owner paying the vet up front and submitting a claim to the insurance company for reimbursement. Companies generally pay 70–90% of the claim submitted, minus any deductible or coinsurance amount.

Range of costs and benefits

In the United States, monthly insurance rates for pet insurance range from USD5.75 per month for a basic policy (USD200 deductible, coverage for accidents; no illness coverage), to USD76.79 per month for a deluxe policy with a low deductible (USD100 deductible; accident and illness coverage to 80%; spaying and neutering covered; essential preventive care; rabies vaccination; free lost pet recovery tag; annual physical exam and dental cleaning; continual coverage for some chronic and long-term conditions that may have arisen in the previous policy year).

You can find all kinds of policies and rates in between these two extremes.

You should be aware that actual premiums may vary depending on your pet's age, breed and where you live.

Keep in mind that most policies allow you to use any vet you like when you have pet insurance. You are usually not limited to using a vet chosen by your pet insurer (though you should check the policy wording).

Pet insurance does help protect you from large, unexpected vet bills that can result from accidents and, in some cases, from illnesses, depending on your policy. However, you must make sure that your policy covers your pet's problem, or potential health problem. Otherwise the policy won't be any use to you. So, if your dog develops cancer and you have a pet insurance policy that doesn't cover cancer, the policy won't pay for anything. This is something to consider before choosing a policy or deciding if you want to get pet insurance.

What to look for in pet insurance cover

These are the costs and features that you look at when considering which cover you'll buy:

- Monthly premium.
- Type of cover it provides (accident, illness, comprehensive).
- Annual limit on claims.
- Excess costs.
- Exclusions (for example if you live in a tick prone area, make sure tick paralysis is part of the policy).
- Extras.
- Age limit on joining. Insurance companies realize that old pets get more problems and so many won't insure pets over the age of 8.

Contact information for pet insurers

The best place to compare policies and get contact information for pet insurers online for Canada, United Kingdom and United States is here. They compare policies, provide information about pet insurance, and link you to reviews given by current customers. A similar online service is available in Australia.

Vaccinations

Vaccinations can be administered at the dog's shoulders (withers) or into the large thigh muscle. There is considerable debate as to how often adult dogs should receive boosters. Many vets administer boosters on an annual basis, although some authorities argue that once every three years is sufficient. Having said that, the correct level and type of vaccinations should be discussed with your vet, as requirements vary between location, breed, lifestyle, health and age. Some owners opt for blood titers, which show the level of immunity in your dog's system, before scheduled vaccinations to see if they're actually necessary.

When should your puppy be vaccinated?

When puppies ingest their mother's milk, they are basically given antibodies that help fight diseases. This immunity starts to fade after six weeks of age. At that time, it is vital that vaccinations are given over a course of 2–3 injections (approximately 3 to 4 weeks apart). After that, vaccines should be given at regular intervals. Vaccine schedules vary and so you should follow the recommended schedule of your vet. Often, the injections are given on an annual basis. This is something you should discuss with your vet when you take your puppy for a checkup after you first pick her up.

How do vaccinations work?

Vaccines work by allowing small amounts of the killed organism into your dog's system, which stimulates your dog's immune system. The immune system sets to work producing cells and proteins to counteract the small amount, which then creates antibodies that protect against the diseases.

Vaccinations cannot be 100% guaranteed. However, vaccinations, along with safe sanitary conditions and good nutrition, are the best protection for your dog.

What are the core vaccinations?

These are some of the diseases against which vets generally recommend vaccination:

> *Canine Distemper* – Often fatal, this is a highly contagious and difficult to treat virus. This disease is spread via discharge from nose and eyes of infected dogs. The virus attacks many organs and can cause permanent damage to the nervous system, even if the dog survives. Symptoms may include: listlessness, fever, coughing, diarrhea and vomiting, with convulsions and coughing heralding the disease's final stages.

Canine Cough – This is a highly contagious respiratory tract infection created by airborne viruses and bacteria. Dogs often catch this disease in places where lots of dogs frequent, such as a boarding kennel (hence the alias 'kennel cough'). The most obvious symptom is a dry, hacking cough.

Canine Parvovirus – This virus is relatively new (emerging in 1978) and is extremely deadly to puppies and unvaccinated adult dogs. This disease is highly contagious and widespread. Symptoms can include lethargy, bloody diarrhea and vomiting.

Canine Hepatitis – This potentially fatal disease can be spread via bodily fluid and secretions such as infected urine, saliva and feces. It can cause liver failure, eye damage and breathing problems.Symptoms may include listlessness, fever, coughing, diarrhea and vomiting.

Rabies – This preventable viral disease is often transmitted between animals (including to humans) via the bite of an infected animal. The rabies virus infects the central nervous system, ultimately causing disease in the brain and death. The early symptoms of rabies in people include fever, headache, and general weakness or discomfort. As the disease progresses symptoms such as insomnia, anxiety, confusion, slight or partial paralysis, excitation, hallucinations, agitation, hyper-salivation (increase in saliva), difficulty swallowing, and hydrophobia (fear of water) may appear. Death usually occurs within days of the onset of these symptoms.

In dogs, early symptoms of rabies can include:

- Fever.
- Lethargy.
- Loss of appetite.
- Odd behavior.

- Changes in bark tone.
- Chewing/attention at the bite site.

Later, symptoms like aggression, biting, constant growling, disorientation, foaming at the mouth and seizures can manifest. In the last stages before death, the dog can exhibit signs of choking, dropping and/or paralysis of the lower jaw.

It's important to note that rabid dogs may not show any one of the above symptoms. So, it's best to stay away from strange dogs. Having said that, countries including New Zealand, United Kingdon, Ireland, Taiwan, Japan, Hawaii, Mauritius, Barbados, and Guam do not have rabies. Although Australia and United Kingdom have rabies amongst their bat populations, rabies vaccinations for dogs are not a requirement in those countries.

Rabies has been eradicated amongst the dog population in the United States as a result of ongoing legally mandated vaccine use. However, rabies is still carried by urban wildlife in North America (such as skunks and bats), so dogs in North American rural and city areas are still vulnerable.

Post vaccination

After a vaccination, most dogs experience no reaction, but some may feel unwell for a few hours. Serious reactions are quite rare. If you notice unusual symptoms within 24 hours of vaccination, call your vet immediately.

Vaccination records

Always keep your vaccinations or blood titer records up to date and easily accessible. You'll need these records for emergency care, training classes, grooming or boarding. If you travel with your dog, keep a copy in the vehicle.

Other ways you can protect your puppy

After your puppy's final injection (of the required 2-3 injections), you should still be careful for several weeks. So avoid these places or activities until your puppy is fully immunized:

- Pet stores.
- Parks and other public places where dogs congregate.
- Animal shelters or kennels.

Diseases can be passed around animal shelters so you should be very careful about any puppy or dog you adopt from a shelter. If you have other dogs at home it's a good idea to try to quarantine your new puppy for the first few days so any disease won't be passed along to other dogs. This may not be possible but it is a good idea.

Controlling Parasites

Worms are essentially parasites. They feed off your dog. Whilst some parasites can cause discomfort, others can have a disastrous effect on our dog's health. Depending on the type of worm and/or intensity of infection, symptoms range from mild discomfort, to diarrhea, nausea, coma and even death.

There are many different ways dogs can become infected with worms or their larvae. Common ways are through eating other dog or cat poop, and coming into contact with other infected dogs, animals, vermin and dirt. This is why it is important to ensure that you give your dog the best level of protection against worms.

In this chapter, I'll discuss two types of worms – intestinal worms and heartworm - and what measures you can take to ensure that your dog is protected against them.

Intestinal Worms

Intestinal worms, in particular, steal much needed nutrients from your dog's digestive system. This, in turn, can leave your dog lacking certain nutrients, which the dog needs for her growth and health. In the dog's digestive system, most nutrients are absorbed in the small intestine, and this is precisely where intestinal worms do their best thieving! Dogs can pick up these worms from ingesting dog and cat poop, and from other infected dogs.

The most common worms are: whipworm, hookworm, roundworm and tapeworm. I'll discuss each of these in turn:

- *Whipworm*

Whipworms actually look like little whips! They get their nutrition by drinking the blood of the host dog. Whipworms are smaller than other intestinal worms, ranging in size between 1 and 2 inches (3–5 cm) in length. Dogs can get infected by eating infected poop or infected dirt (as whipworm eggs can live in dirt).

How can you tell if your dog has whipworm?

Whipworms can cause recurring diarrhea (which may be bloody), weight loss, anemia and colitis (inflammation of the large intestine). Whipworms are hard to detect as dogs do not generally display symptoms, however when the infestation is serious, visible signs may include bloody poop, weight loss, dehydration and anemia.

Whipworm – the bottom line:

Whipworm is not generally life threatening, however it can cause significant discomfort. Having said that, on rare occasions when severe infestation occurs, death can come about as a result of dehydration and anemia.

- *Roundworm*

Many puppies are born with roundworm as these worms pass from the dam to the puppy prior to birth or during whelping. Puppies and adult dogs can also catch roundworm by eating infected poop or vermin (such as rodents).

In adult dogs, roundworm larvae can infest the respiratory system and lay dormant in other organs, only to resurface many years later. In younger dogs, the larvae live in the respiratory system and are regurgitated.

Once regurgitated, the dog reinitiates the cycle by eating its own vomit, thereby allowing roundworm to mature in the intestinal system from which it is passed with the feces.

How can you tell if your dog has Roundworm?

Roundworms can cause diarrhea and vomiting in adult dogs and puppies. Dogs may just look unhealthy or have a pot-belly appearance. They may also pass whole roundworms in their poop. You can see these worms in your dog's poop: they are approximately 2 to 4 inches (5–12.5 cm) long, spaghetti-like and white.

Roundworm – the bottom line:

Roundworm is not generally life threatening, however it can cause discomfort.

- *Hookworm*

Hookworms can enter the body through the skin or by being swallowed. Once inside they settle in the dog's small intestine or lungs. Just like whipworms, hookworms feed on the dog's blood rather than on the nutrients that pass through the system.

How can you tell if your dog has hookworm?

Hookworms can cause itchy feet, a rash on the dog's feet, coughing and wheezing, diarrhea, abdominal cramps, nausea, and bloody or black poop. In advanced cases, hookworms can cause anemia and death. Puppies are particularly vulnerable and can die if infected.

Hookworm – the bottom line:

Hookworms are difficult to detect and can be life-threatening. Consult your veterinarian for regular testing, especially if you don't use a preventative.

- *Tapeworm*

Tapeworms live in a dog's small intestine and absorb the nutrients there. Dogs can get tapeworms by eating an infected flea whilst self-grooming or licking their coat. Tapeworms can grow to about 15 feet (about 4.5 metres) long, however they shed in segments ranging from ¼ to ½ inch (1–1.5 cm) long. The segments can be found in your dog's poop.

How can you tell if your dog has tapeworm?

Symptoms include abdominal discomfort, nervousness, itching around the anus, vomiting and weight loss. The itching may result in your dog 'scooting' her bum along the ground. Segments of tapeworm can be found in your dog's poop. The segments are small, wide and flat and look like grains of uncooked rice or sesame seeds.

Tapeworm – the bottom line:

Tapeworm is not life threatening, however it can cause discomfort.

The prevention of intestinal worms

There are a number of easy, inexpensive measures you can take to prevent your dog from becoming infected by intestinal worms. They are:

- Ask your vet for a 'broad-spectrum' worming preventative. This will protect your dog against heartworms, roundworms, whipworms, hookworms and, depending on which medication you use, even fleas. No preventative can offer 100% protection, however, properly administering the monthly tablet on time, is the best protection you can give your dog.
- If getting a new puppy, ask the breeder or the puppy's seller, whether your puppy had commenced with a worming preventative at about two weeks of age.
- Keep your dog's area clean and remove poop regularly.
- Keep your dog from eating wild animals and vermin as they can be infected with worms.

- Keep your dog from eating animal carcasses such as birds, rodents and rabbits.
- Dogs should not be allowed to eat offal from any animal.
- Ensure that the areas and parks that your dog visits are clean and well maintained – raise this issue with relevant municipalities, if necessary.
- As part of your dog's annual check-up, have your vet conduct an examination of your dog's poop.
- Ensure your dog's toys, bones and chewy items are relatively free of dirt.

The treatment of intestinal worms

If your dog is infected or has not being given a worming preventative,

consult your vet. Treatment is very important, and any treatment of worms in dogs should be repeated over time to effectively kill all live and dormant larvae and eggs. Treatment usually involves de-wormer medication. Even if you find a de-wormer that does not require a prescription, you should still use it under your veterinarian's supervision. This is because doses can vary depending on your dog's size and the severity of the infection. Your vet will be able to tell you what dosage is right for your dog.

Heartworm

Heartworm is a parasitic disease that is spread by mosquitoes, so all dogs are vulnerable. These long, spaghetti-like worms infest the dog's heart and can grow to anywhere between 6 and 10 inches (17–27 cm)

long. This disease can also affect cats, ferrets, foxes, wolves, sea lions and horses.

Heartworm is a serious condition and should be considered in any preventative worming regimen.

How can you tell if your dog has heartworm?

Most dogs do not show any symptoms until several years after the initial infection, by which time the disease has progressed to an advanced stage. Chronic infection can cause loss of appetite, weight loss, lethargy, intolerance to exercise, coughing and breathing difficulties. Acute infection can result in shock, vomiting, diarrhea and fainting.

Cases of heartworm that are advanced and untreated can kill a dog within 3 days of symptoms appearing. If you suspect your dog is infected, take her to a vet immediately.

How can you prevent heartworm in your dog?

In order to ensure your dog does not become infected by heartworm, you have two options: the first is a monthly tablet (or chew) and the second is an annual injection (given by a vet). No preventative can offer

100% protection, however, properly administering the monthly tablet or annual injection on time, is the best protection you can give your dog.

Annual injections do away with the need to remember monthly doses. It is important to enter the annual injection appointments into your diary so that there is no gap in coverage. Some vets will send you a letter before each yearly injection is due, however it is best not to rely on this as your sole reminder.

What if your dog has never received any heartworm prevention?

Before starting a monthly dose or annual injection, ask your vet to perform a simple test to confirm your dog is free of the disease. This is necessary because heartworm preventative works best and will not cause further health issues if the dog is free of heartworm.

Heartworm treatment for an infected dog

The best course of action for the treatment of an infected dog is best discussed with your vet. Treatment options can include injections and, in severe cases, surgical removal of the worms might be necessary. Both options can be risky and even dangerous to dogs that already have other pre-existing conditions such as disease of the liver or kidneys.

Heartworm – the bottom line:

This parasite can be fatal, if left unchecked. If you have any concerns about your dog and you suspect heartworm you should see your vet immediately.

3 Things You Must Know Regarding The Monthly Prevention Of Heartworm and intestinal Worms

If you choose to give your dog a monthly tablet as a preventative against heartworm or intestinal worms, and to afford your dog the best protection, make sure you:

1. Give monthly doses on the same date each month. Irregular doses can reduce the effectiveness of the coverage.
   There is a margin of error, so if follow these guidelines if you have forgotten to give your dog a monthly dose on schedule:
   - If you are up to 15 days late, immediately dose your dog and continue with the original dosing schedule.
   - If you are between 15-30 days late, immediately dose your dog and ensure that doses are administered on time for at least the next two months to ensure complete protection.
   - If you are more than 60 days late in administering a dose, consult your vet immediately.
2. Ensure that the correct dose is given according to your dog's weight. The required dosage amount per month will depend upon your dog's weight. Therefore, consult your vet or the pamphlet provided with the drugs for the correct dosage guidelines.
3. Set reminders for heartworm and intestinal worm prevention. Apart from adding the dates in advance to your diary, you can take advantage of a free monthly email or text message reminder service offered by many drug companies when you buy their product.

How to Give Your Dog a Pill

There are a few ways to give your dog a pill. You can always hide the pill in their food. Some dogs will eat the food along with the pill. While other dogs will be able to separate the food and pill; they then eat all the food and ignore the pill!

If your dog dislikes pills, you can always administer pills to your dog manually in four easy steps:

1. Kneel beside your dog and gently squeeze your dog's mouth open with your thumb and middle finger of your left hand.
2. With your right hand, push the pill as far back into the dog's mouth as possible.
3. Now gently keep your dog's mouth closed with your left hand and rub your dog's throat with your right hand to stimulate the dog's impulse to swallow (see picture below). Ensure your dog has swallowed at least two-three times before releasing your dog.
4. Watch your dog for a few moments, just to make sure she does not regurgitate the pill.

If giving pills to multiple dogs at the same time, watch them closely, as some dogs see pills as treats and may steal them from their fellow pack members.

Fleas

If your dog is constantly scratching herself, then she might have fleas.

Fleas can be a year-long pest, but tend to have less chance of survival in colder climates.

You can check if your dog has fleas by combing through her fur with a fine-toothed comb. Use a white piece of kitchen towel or tissue to collect any debris and dirt that is caught with the comb. Carefully moisten the tissue with water. Any debris that dissolves into a reddish-brown, rust-colored stain is flea poop or the digested blood of your dog.

Even if you find one flea, or only one of your dogs has fleas, chances are there are hundreds about. So, treat all your dogs with spot treatment and wash (or replace) all bedding and blankets.

You can purchase 'spot' preventatives from your vet. These spot treatments are put directly on the skin between the shoulder blades (withers) and disperse throughout the skin, without entering the dog's blood stream. You may have to shave a small area to apply the spot treatment for dogs with very heavy coats.

If fleas are an ongoing problem, then you may have to consider treating your house for fleas.

Flea treatments for dogs are potentially fatal to cats, so don't use canine flea control on your cats. You must use a cat specific flea control for your felines.

Flea Allergies

The most common allergy in dogs is the flea allergy. The mere presence of fleas and their bites can cause any dog to itch, but with flea allergies the symptoms are much more severe. A dog that has a flea allergy can suffer severe bouts of itching from just one single bite. Often, a dog will be severely itchy despite there being no actual evidence of fleas on the dog. Dogs suffering from flea allergy react to substances in the saliva of the flea. When the flea bites its saliva is transferred into the dog's blood stream and causes the itch. Only your vet can make the final diagnosis, but if your dog experiences severe itching as described above, with redness and dryness of the skin, then a flea allergy should be considered even if your dog has been treated for fleas.

Ticks

Ticks are a blood sucking parasite that lives off an animal. There are hundreds of species of ticks worldwide. In North America, the most common ticks are deer tick, brown dog tick, lone star tick and American dog tick. Most flea spot treatments also repel ticks, but there is no current vaccine for the tick's toxin. Ticks can potentially transmit diseases, such as Lyme disease, ehrlichiosis, Rocky Mountain spotted fever, anaplasmosis and babesiosis. However, many are without disease. The symptoms of most tick-borne diseases include fever and lethargy, and others cause weakness, lameness, joint swelling and anemia.

Dogs in Australia can be vulnerable to paralysis ticks. Symptoms of tick paralysis include: appetite loss, vomiting or dry retching, excessive salivation, difficulty swallowing, difficulty breathing, coughing, changes to the dog's bark, noisy panting and difficulty swallowing. In the latter stages your dog may experience weakened limbs, incontinence, paralysis and coma.

There are many species of ticks in different parts of the world. If you are worried about whether there is a tick problem in your area or you are considering travelling with your dog, ask your vet about this.

Tick prevention

Here are three ways to prevent a tick attaching itself to your dog:

1. Keep your garden area trimmed and mown.
2. Treat outdoor areas with a pet and environmentally friendly pesticide.
3. Apply a monthly tick prevention product directly onto your dog. Or you can use a tick collar.

What to do if your dog has a tick

Keep your dog as calm as possible. Remove food and water as the dog may choke if she is experiencing difficulty swallowing. Remove the tick, if you can. Take your dog to the vet immediately.

This is how you can remove your tick:

1. Wear latex gloves to protect yourself and use a pair of tweezers. There are also specialty tick removal tools that you may be able to purchase at pet supply stores or online.
2. Use tweezers to grasp the tick at the point where it has attached itself to your dog, as close to the dog's skin as possible.
3. Do not squeeze the body of the tick, as this may cause bacteria and disease to be injected into the dog.
4. Carefully pull the tick straight out from the skin; this must be done steadily, slowly and without twisting or turning the tick. It's normal for some of your dog's skin to come off with the tick.
5. Once removed, the tick should either be flushed down the toilet or placed in a small container so you can show your vet.
6. After tick removal, clean your dog's skin at the bite area with mild soap and water. If your dog is bleeding, apply light pressure. Do not apply any type of alcohol (including methylated spirits), lit or hot matches, nail polish, petroleum jelly or chemicals to the area – this may cause more harm to your dog.

Skin Issues

Warts

Puppy warts are caused by the canine papilloma virus. Warts are not typically considered to be serious. Some people refer to this as the doggie chicken pox because it can look a little like human chicken pox.

Puppy warts appear as small lumps and are often found in the dog's mouth. They can look like a little cauliflower or a raspberry. They are not cancerous and will often go unnoticed unless you brush your puppy's teeth or your vet notices them up during a check-up.

Puppy warts are passed on to your puppy from other infected dogs. They may be picked up in kennels, the vet's office, during puppy classes or at dog parks. The warts cannot be transmitted from your puppy to humans or even other animals.

If you notice warts in your dog's mouth, see a vet to ensure that the warts don't interfere with the puppy's eating habits. Provided there are no problems with the puppy eating, no treatment is necessary. The warts will heal in their own time. Once she has had the condition, a full immunity will develop and she will not have this condition again unless her immune system is weakened as a result of another illness or disease.

Extreme cases can be cause for concern. A puppy with an abundance of warts might have a weak immune system. If the warts hinder the dog's ability to eat, drink or breathe, they might have to be surgically removed.

Other skin disorders

Skin problems are common in dogs and can be attributed to one or more causes including allergies, mites and autoimmune disease. They can also result from serious underlying issues such as glandular diseases, cancer, a malfunctioning thyroid and Cushing's syndrome (a hormone disorder caused by high levels of cortisol in the blood).

With skin problems, a visit to the vet for a biopsy examination of the dog's skin culture may result in diagnosis. However, a visit to a dermatologist may be required if the vet's efforts to diagnose and treat a skin problem are unsuccessful. Unfortunately, some skin problems can be quite tricky to diagnose and treat. When discussing your dog's condition, discuss the possibility of fish (or other) supplements, dietary changes, medicated shampoos and steroid injections.

Fungal problems

Fungal skin problems are often found in dogs with allergies (for more information about allergies, see the next section). Some fungus is highly contagious (like ringworm), whilst others – such as yeast – are not transmitted as easily. Fungal skin infections can manifest as either crusty red lumps or red and black swollen skin. They can have a similar appearance to mange, and the dog will also have a distinctive, strong odor.

Mange

Mange is a contagious skin disease caused by parasiticnites. This condition presents as flaky skin, bald patches and itching. Several types of mites can be passed to humans (a human infection is known as scabies). Diagnosis of mange can be difficult, particularly with one type of mite (sarcoptic) as their already relatively low numbers may be removed by the dog's chewing.

There are three ways in which mange might be diagnosed:

(i) The simplest and most common method is via the *Pedal-Pinnareflex* which is when the dog engages one of its hind legs in a scratching motion as the vet gently scratches and manipulates her ear.

(ii) Examination of a skin culture under a microscope.

(iii) A serologic test, which is available in some countries.

Bacterial infections

A dog's skin may become infected after it has been compromised and damaged by an underlying health issue or via the actions of the dog when dealing with itching (such as incessant scratching and chewing). In these cases, your vet may recommend antibiotics.

Allergies

There are four types of canine allergies – food, fleas, inhalants (such as dust, mould, different grasses or pollen) and contact allergies to chemical. Inhalant allergies are more common than food allergies, with only 10% of allergic reactions being attributed to food. Contact allergies to chemicals are quite rare, but should be considered if diagnosis proves difficult. Flea allergies were discussed above.

Often food allergies are caused by the carbohydrates and starch used in the food, for example wheat, grain and rice. Other dogs react to proteins, displaying beef and chicken allergies for instance. Soy allergies are very common. Fish allergies are rare, as are allergies to rarer animal protein such as bison or deer.

Some breeds are more prone to allergies, including bulldogs, retrievers, poodles and some terriers. A predisposition to allergies is often genetic, so dogs with allergy prone parents might be affected too.

Symptoms for canine allergies may include:

- Intense itching – this is the most common symptom. Dogs may use their paws or an object to rub their face or torso, or they may scoot their hind along the ground.
- Raw skin – this is a result of the dog chewing the affected area. Flea allergies may result in the dog chewing her hindquarters raw.
- Hot spots – these are localized rashes that can feel very warm to the touch. They commonly appear on the shoulder or on the hind quarter of the dog.

- Visible rash – inhalant and food allergies may also result in itch, reddened feet.
- Watery, red eyes.
- Frequent ear and bladder infections and increased susceptibility to illness – this is because the dog's skin is damaged and bacteria are allowed to thrive.
- Vomiting and diarrhea – food allergies may lead to the symptoms listed above, but they may also manifest in this way.

When talking to your vet about possible allergy treatments, remember the following points:

- There is no real cure for an allergy – just prevention and relief.
- The source of any allergy is often difficult to identify. The possibility of a flea allergy should be considered even if your dog has been treated for fleas. However, using flea preventatives will help reduce the likelihood of flea allergy.
- In severe cases, steroids can be used to lessen symptoms of flea allergies, but in the long term steroids can suppress the immune system.
- Food allergies are identified through elimination diets, undertaken under the supervision of your vet.
- Your discussion with your vet should be centered on managing the symptoms.
- Your vet may be able to procure a culture from the affected skin, to see what type of medication can be prescribed.
- Antihistamine may be a good idea to reduce symptoms. Your vet can talk to you about whether this is appropriate and in what dosages.
- You could be referred to a canine dermatologist who may be able to isolate the cause and prescribe injections that will alleviate the symptoms. This option is more expensive, however.
- Vaccinations that are given too often may make an allergic response worse, so consider discussing the frequency of vaccinations and the use of blood titers.

When it comes to managing allergies there are many things you can do at home to lessen the symptoms:

- Itchy skin can be soothed by using medicated or oatmeal shampoo and supplements like fish oil capsules.
- Keep your dog's ears clean to prevent a buildup of yeast.
- Cranberries or cranberry supplements can help prevent bladder infections (that may arise from food allergies).
- Use an air purifier in the home.
- Wash your dog's bedding regularly.
- Keep the house vacuumed and use natural, non-toxic cleaners.

Joint Problems

Dogs have about 320 bones in their bodies, compared to 206 for humans. The actual number of bones depends on whether the dog has dew claws (located on the inside leg above the paw) and the length of the dog's tail.

To help your puppy's growing bones develop properly, make sure the puppy avoids stressing her bones or joints with activities such as jumping or strenuous exercise until she's fully grown.

Signs of joint pain

If you notice your puppy or adult dog showing the following signs, then your dog may be suffering from joint pain:

- Stiffness.
- Lameness.
- Abnormal, hesitant or labored gait.
- Favoring a limb.
- Difficulty sitting or standing.
- Hesitant to get up.
- Difficulty with climbing stairs.
- Yelping when moving or stopping.
- 'Bunny-hopping' type movements.

The most common ailments that can cause joint pain are:

- Arthritis.
- Elbow and hip dysplasia.
- Slipping knee joints (luxating patellas).

Arthritis is an inflammation of any joint or spine; it can cause pain and swelling. Arthritis is most common in older dogs, but hip or elbow dysplasia can also lead to early onset arthritis.

Dysplasia can be first noticed in puppies under one year old. Hip and elbow dysplasia are common in dogs, more so in larger breeds. Mixed breeds, purebreds and dogs of both genders can be affected by dysplasia, with more males affected by elbow dysplasia. Dysplasia is hereditary, but you might be able to avoid it by staying clear of breeds that are commonly affected; certain breeds such as the German Shepherd are known for hip dysplasia. Choosing a responsible, certified breeder can help avoid this issue – ask if the parents of the relevant litter have been certified to be free from dysplasia. As dysplasia is genetic, it is unlikely that your dog will be affected if both her parents are free from the disease.

Slipping knee joints can affect any dog, but toy breeds tend to be more susceptible. A slipping knee cap is a common problem that affects dogs of all ages and sizes. In affected dogs, the knee cap is not held securely against the joint but rather floats along the leg.

If you suspect your dog to be suffering from joint pain, have her examined by a vet who will be able to make an accurate diagnosis via gentle movement of all joints (to check for range of movement as well as pain) and x-rays. Just be aware that elbow dysplasia can be more difficult to diagnose.

Treatments for the causes of joint pain

Treatment options should be discussed with your vet because they will depend on the vet's preferences as well your dog's age, health, your budget and the type of condition your dog suffers from.

Treatment options range from simply modifying the dog's exercise and activities to supplements, medication for easing pain, and surgery.

Here are some things to note when you are discussing these options with your vet:

- Mild cases of dysplasia, slipping knee joints or arthritis may not require surgery. However, severe cases may require surgical intervention. If your vet recommends surgery, get a second opinion from an orthopedist, who will have up-to-date information on available medications and procedures.
- A total hip replacement is the most common surgery for dealing with hip dysplasia. This surgery includes removing the entire joint and then replacing it with a synthetic hip. Hip replacements can only be undertaken once the dog has finished growing, and there is usually a two to three month wait between replacing the two hips. Femoral head and neck excision is a procedure in which the head and neck of the thigh bone is removed. This is a relatively easy and cheap procedure and can work well in dogs under 20kgs (44lbs). The range of movement and the stability of the hip that can be achieved with this procedure is not as good as it is with other procedures, but can be satisfactory. The vet will suggest that the dog is given limited exercise and a low calorie diet after the surgery, but once the dog has healed, she will be allowed to exercise as before. Limiting her weight will help to reduce any complications that she may otherwise experience.
- Any surgical procedure requires follow up attention with the dog's vet, along with physiotherapy in many cases. Pet physiotherapists can be very helpful with building the muscles and pain management.
- Your vet may also recommend pain medications. Drugs won't correct the condition, but they can significantly reduce pain, inflammation and stiffness. In the long term, pain killers (also known as anti-inflammatory drugs) can have significant side effects, such as stomach ulcers and kidney failure. So, monitor the length of the dog's drug usage in consultation with your vet.

Unless they are time release capsules, you can make giving your dog pills easier by dissolving them in water or grinding them up and mixing them with the dog's food. You could also use a pill-gun or pet-piller which works by 'injecting' the pill into your dog's mouth.

- At no time should you consider giving your dog pain medications meant for humans. Aspirin, for example, is not suitable for dogs, and dosages for pain medications that are considered appropriate for people can prove quite deadly for dogs.

- Many supplements are available from veterinarians and over the counter that can help to reduce the effects of inflammation seen with arthritis. Glucosamine extracted from green lip mussels, for example, can be very effective without the long-term side effects of pain killers. Supplements do not reverse arthritis, but they can slow down the process. Supplements such as glucosamine and chondroitin are commonly prescribed to dogs with hip dysplasia. These supplements help to repair cartilage in the joint and support the lubrication of the joint. Better lubrication means less pain and less destruction of the joint. The supplements are easy to obtain and are often sold over the counter at your local pet supply store, but their effectiveness varies widely.

- Most joint support supplements made for humans are fine for dogs too, as they contain the same active ingredients.

- Alternative forms of treatment for arthritis may include gold implants and acupuncture. Some vets are certified acupuncturists.

- An exercise regimen that encourages a slow and steady pace suits dogs with joint pain best, whereas abrupt stopping and starting motions should be discouraged. This includes mounting and descending stairs (if it can be avoided), jumping out of the boot of the car and throwing sticks or balls (as this means your dog will start, stop and turn abruptly). Consider exercises such as swimming as the weightlessness helps build up the muscles without placing stress on the joint and tendons. Pet physiotherapists may be able to provide access to special dog pools, some with underwater treadmills. Frequent, gentle exercise also serves to increase muscle mass which also helps to reduce the stress that joints experience.

- If your dog is carrying too much weight, losing the excess weight should be your first priority. This is because too much weight places extra stress on your dog's joints. Weight loss can have a massive impact on reducing pain.

- Perna mussels are edible shell fish that are known for assisting with joint health. This shell fish has a high level of glycosaminoglycans (GAG's) which are known to assist in the formation and repair of connective materials within the joints. This makes it an ideal fish for dogs (and people) that have arthritis and hip dysplasia problems. Unsaponifiables are components in avocados and soybeans which are thought to help rebuild cartilage and prevent arthritis pain and degradation.

- Polysulfated glycosaminoglycan can also be injected directly into the joints on a weekly or monthly basis. This treatment is thought to help rebuild the cartilage within the hips. It is injected directly into the muscles surrounding the joints. The treatment has a good track record, often providing promising results.

Chapter 9: The Sure-Fire Way to Get Your Puppy Potty Trained In a Week

Potty training is the first thing you teach your puppy. A new owner's biggest frustration is the fact that puppies have no clue where to do their business! This chapter gives you clear, easy to follow steps and tips which will make the process easier. If issues around toilet training persist for a long time, consider seeking veterinary advice to make sure your puppy has no bladder or other health problems.

In this chapter, I'll explain:

- The three basic rules of quick and easy potty training.
- The potty schedule which will help you know when your puppy is likely to potty.
- How to train your puppy to use a crate.
- Tell-tale signs your puppy is about to potty.
- How to handle accidents.
- Ways you can reinforce good behavior, so your puppy learns to potty outside faster.

Three Basic Rules of Potty Training

Your goal as a puppy owner is to ensure that your puppy learns to potty outside as quickly as possible. This means that your puppy should have as few opportunities as possible to potty inside. Three basic rules apply when you are teaching your puppy to potty outside:

- Set your puppy up for success.
- Recognizing when your dog needs to toilet.
- Reward and punish your dog the correct way.

1. Set your puppy up for success

The more success and the more rewarded your puppy feels, the more likely your dog will develop confidence and learn to potty outside quickly.

Puppies – especially toy breeds – do not have full control over their bladders until they are between five to seven months old. Therefore, it's up to you to ensure they are outside at the right times.

The easy option

Ideally, keep your puppy outside for most of the day so the puppy will naturally learn to go outside. This is an especially good tactic if you don't mind where in the backyard your puppy decides to potty.

Follow this timetable

If you prefer to keep puppy inside with you, then I have devised this simple timetable to help you know when to take your puppy outside to potty:

	Potty Time
Throughout the night	Take puppy outside to potty if you hear she is awake
6am	Take puppy outside for the day's first potty
Throughout the day	Waking up – take puppy outside shortly afterwards Drinking – take puppy outside shortly afterwards Play or Training – take puppy outside shortly afterwards
Eating	Take puppy outside for a poop 30 minutes later. Eating schedule for puppies is: • 7 weeks through 4 months is 4 times a day • 4 to 7 months is 3 times a day • 7 months onwards is 2 times a day
6pm	Stop food after this time to limit poop
11.30pm or late as possible	Last potty outside before bedtime

Crate training

In between these times, you can confine your dog to a crate for short periods. Puppies have been taught by their mother (dam) not to soil their sleeping area. This effectively means that puppies have been toilet trained since about three weeks old. When you first bring your puppy home, it's your job to continue with this training. This means that their sleeping area should be small enough so they do not want to soil it. Having said that, if you keep a puppy in a crate for too long then the puppy may be forced to potty in it and once this happens your puppy may start to develop the undesirable habit of peeing inside her crate.

Puppies can: (i) be naughty at times; (ii) be destructive and messy in the house; and (iii) sleep a lot after they use up their energy. Crate training is a good solution for some of your puppy's less desirable behaviors such as chewing and house soiling. It also keeps her out of trouble when you can't be home. And being crated can provide your puppy with a safe place to sleep and rest.

Purchase a crate that will be large enough for your puppy when she's an adult. Most manufacturers give good guidance regarding which crate is right for each breed (or mix) so check the labels or tags. When in doubt, get a crate that is a little larger rather than one that's too small. However, don't get an enormous crate that will be too big for your dog when she's full-grown. Dogs generally like to feel well-insulated and comforted in their crates, like a den. They won't feel safe in a huge space.

If you choose an adult sized crate for your puppy, then fill the extra space with blankets - this way the dog will not soil the crate as they do not like to pee or poop in their living space. If the crate is too big, the puppy may use the crate as a potty, which is exactly the behavior you are trying to discourage!

There are several different kinds of crates: hard plastic airline crates, wire crates, and canvas crates. There are even wicker crates and other unusual crates. They are all fine for different purposes, although canvas, wicker and other crates are usually not a good choice for a puppy since they are easily torn or chewed. I recommend you choose a hard plastic or wire crate for crate training.

It's not hard to crate train a puppy but your puppy may complain about it at first, depending on her early experiences with a crate. Some breeders use a crate as part of their whelping set-up so some puppies are used to them from birth. They have no objection to spending time in a crate or sleeping in one. To them a crate is a cozy, safe place that they associate with their mother and littermates.

Other puppies, however, may not have seen a crate before. Initially, at least, they may think of being in the crate as jail time. Since you may not know whether your puppy has any experience with a crate it's always a good idea to introduce the crate slowly.

Three steps to easy crate training:

1. Allow your puppy to explore the crate.

    Once you have the right crate you should place it in a spot in your home where your puppy can explore it. Leave the door wide open. Place a comfortable sheepskin mat or some towels in the crate and put some treats and toys inside. Many puppies will go inside to get the treats. Your puppy may decide to take a nap there. That's fine - you should let her sleep there with the door open. Let her get used to going in and out of the crate as she likes. You can also begin feeding your puppy dinner in the crate, with the door open.

2. Introduce short periods of crate time.

    After your puppy has become used to the crate you can start closing the door for short periods of time while you are home with her. Close the door for a couple of minutes and give your puppy something good to chew on while she's in the crate. Some puppies may not notice that you have closed the door. They will be focused on the chewie. Other puppies may protest about the closed door. It is best to open the door after a couple of minutes and let your puppy out when the puppy is quiet. Do this a few times each day for several days. You can gradually keep your puppy in the crate for longer periods of time, always making sure that you are home with her.

Your puppy should begin to get used to spending some time in the crate. Make sure you always give her something safe to occupy her whilst she's in the crate. You should not expect her to spend long periods of time in the crate at this stage, especially if she's very young as she may soil her space or become distressed.

Eventually you can practice going outside for a few minutes while your puppy is in the crate. Your puppy may howl but you will need to ignore it. Then, once settled, you can go back inside and let her out. The key is not to make a fuss when you let your puppy out. In this way she will not become too excited when you return; your puppy will therefore learn that you will always come back and she will not fret whilst you are away.

3. Gradually increase crate time.

    You can gradually leave your puppy for longer periods in the crate while you are absent. If your puppy whinges, howls or freaks out, then cut the time she is left in the crate by half and slowly build up the absences as your puppy remains calmly in her crate. When your puppy is still quite young, remember that she will need to be toileted frequently so ensure she is let out often. If she soils her crate this may lead to a bad habit that is hard to break.

    If you follow these suggestions your puppy will be crate trained in just a few weeks. Some puppies learn faster than others. Some puppies will calm down and take a nap when you leave while others may bark and object at first. The keys are to ensure: (i) your puppy knows that you will return; (ii) the crate is a pleasant place (never scold or punish her whilst she's in her crate); and (iii) you do not make a big fuss when you leave and return.

Controlling your puppy's environment

Giving your puppy the run of the house means you will have less chance of being able to potty train your dog effectively. Limiting the space to which your puppy has access means your puppy won't be able to sneak into an unsupervised room and potty. A great way to ensure your dog is safe, comfortable  and under your supervision is to use an exercise-pen (also known as an x-pen, see picture). By making sure it is near where you and your family hang out in the house, your puppy will feel involved and occupied too. Make sure there are toys and a water bowl in the pen when your dog is using it.

2. Recognizing when your dog needs to toilet

Knowing your puppy's schedule for potty is important, however your puppy may need to go at other times. Puppies usually signal their need to potty by circling and sniffing the ground. However, some puppies may exhibit different signals, so observe your puppy and watch for patterns.

When you think your puppy is about to potty inside, pick her up promptly but gently and take her outside. Be careful not to press your hands against your puppy's abdomen as you do this. Doing this calmly and swiftly means you won't startle your puppy into eliminating whilst she is being carried.

Once you have taken your puppy outside you can have a 'designated area' where you encourage the puppy to go. Choose a patch of garden away from the house, perhaps beneath some trees or shrubs. Initially, your puppy may tend to wander away from the 'designated area'. I recommend taking your puppy out on a leash; so your puppy can also get used being on a leash whilst she is potty training.

You can also place a 'pee post' (available in pet stores) in the 'designated area'. This pheromone infused stake will then encourage your dog to potty in that vicinity.

Puppies are adorable, inquisitive creatures and so they may test your patience by wanting to explore the surroundings without doing what you've taken her outside for. If your puppy does not potty within ten minutes of taking her outside, then bring her back in, crate her and try again in 15 minutes.

3.Reward and punish your dog the correct way

Despite your best efforts, accidents will happen. This is okay and is just part of the process – even seasoned dog trainers experience this with their own dogs! I am often asked by puppy owners what they should do if they catch their puppy eliminating inside.

My advice is not to punish your puppy. This is because your puppy may think that the act of potty itself is what is angering you, so she will then hide the evidence by eliminating behind furniture or beneath curtains. The best reaction is to simply say "whoops" or "d'oh!" then quickly and quietly take your puppy outside. Remember: there's no point punishing your puppy after the fact, because she just won't know why she is being punished.

Make sure you clean up any accidents as quickly as possible. You can use an ammonia-free cleaner (dogs are particularly attracted to peeing on ammonia) or a mixture of water and vinegar. Some household cleaners are not strong enough to actually remove the odor (they merely disguise it), so I suggest asking your vet to recommend an enzyme-based cleaner to get rid of the smell completely.

The general rule is that puppies can only hold their bladder for one hour for each month of age. Therefore, an eight-week-old (two-month-old) puppy can only hold her bladder for two hours. This means there may be accidents at night, unless you are prepared to get up in the middle of the night and toilet her. If you do not intend to toilet your puppy at night, it's best to provide her with 'pee pads' (these are floor napkins available at pet stores) or a litter tray; in this way your puppy does not soil her bedding. It's relatively difficult to wean a puppy off soiling her bed once it starts, so make sure you discourage this.

What to do when your puppy toilets outside

When you have taken your dog outside to the 'designated area', do not play with her or give treats to her until she has toileted.

You can use treats and play as a reward. Make sure your puppy really knows how pleased you are that she has toileted outside – this will increase the chances that she will seek to potty outside next time.

As your dog toilets say a special word, so your puppy learns to potty on command. People tend to use either "potty", "wee", "busy", "go do wee wee" or "toilees". You must say the word just as she begins to potty and only say it once. Timing is the key to teaching a new command, so there is no point saying the word after your dog has finished eliminating. You can choose your own word – just be mindful of choosing a word that you do not mind saying in earshot of others at a park or other public place!

If your puppy is quite stubborn about toileting after being taken outside, here is a trick that might help. Leave your puppy outside and return inside alone. Watch your puppy from inside the house and when she toilets, swing open the door, say "good dog!" and let her back inside. There's no bigger reward for a puppy than to be reunited with her owner. Repeat this process at the next scheduled potty – you'll see your puppy will catch on very quickly!

Remember to use biodegradable poop scoop baggies to clean up after your puppy, especially if she toilets in a public area. You might want to leave some of her poop in your designated area to encourage her to potty in that spot again.

Some people have recommended getting poop from another dog and placing this in the designated area. I highly recommend that you do notdo this: puppies that have not yet had their full course of vaccinations may be vulnerable to possible diseases lurking in another dog's poop.

Your Potty Training Checklist

- Take your puppy outside to potty shortly after waking, sleeping, playing, training and drinking.
- Take your puppy outside to potty 30 minutes after eating.
- Confine your puppy to a crate or exercise pen (x-pen) for short periods.
- Watch for your puppy's potty signals, then gently and promptly take her outside.
- Have a designated spot outside for potty.
- Do not punish your puppy for accidents.
- Give lots of praise when your puppy toilets outside.
- As your dog beings to potty, say "potty" or another special word, so this command is reinforced.

Chapter 10: How You Can Avoid Nasty Hazards to Keep Your Puppy Safe and Apply First Aid in Emergencies

Two of the biggest concerns dog owners have about their pet's safety are:

1. Have I done everything I can to make sure my dog is protected?
2. How do I know when an incident requires an immediate visit to the vet?

Knowing how to safeguard your dog against obvious and hidden dangers and knowing what to do in a variety of situations if your dog is injured are your two best defenses against hazards. The good news is this chapter will explain many easy things you can do to protect your dog and to be prepared for different kinds of emergencies.

It is strongly recommended you familiarize yourself with the contents of this chapter regularly so you are always prepared with the right equipment and able to act quickly in an emergency situation.A book cannot accurately diagnose and propose effective treatments for any condition. Therefore, when in doubt, consult your vet.

In this chapter, I'll explain:

- What to do if your dog stops breathing or is vomiting.
- What to do if your dog is bleeding, or has been run over by a vehicle or been in a fight.
- What to do if your dog is bitten by a snake.
- What to do if your dog is dry-retching or vomiting.
- How to bandage your dog's ear, tail or leg.
- Which 20 poisonous foods to avoid.
- What to do if your dog has eaten poison.
- What to do if your dog has eaten chocolate.
- What to pack in your dog's first aid and evacuation kits.
- How to handle your dog's heat stroke or heat exhaustion.
- How to give your dog a pill.
- The tell-tale signs of shock and how to manage a dog in shock.

Obvious Signs Your Dog Needs Veterinary Attention

If any of the following occur to your dog, you should contact your vet *immediately*:

- The dog has been involved in a car accident or has been run over by a vehicle (car, motor bike or bicycle).
- The dog has been fighting with, or has been bitten by, a snake.
- The dog is suffering convulsions.

- The dog has ingested poison, such as anti-freeze, rat or mouse poison, or has eaten an animal that has been poisoned. Common poisons are listed later in this chapter.
- The dog is suffering from signs of shock (which may manifest in one or more of the following ways):
  - Panting.
  - Shivering.
  - Drooling.
  - Vocalization (whimpering, yelping).
  - Hiding.
  - Reluctance to move or walk.
  - Very dark or very pale or bluish gums.
  - Cold feet.
- The dog is displaying an extreme and sudden mood swing, such as uncharacteristic aggression, timidity or agitation.
- The dog is extremely listless or lethargic.
- The dog is experiencing difficulty breathing, or is gasping or choking.
- The dog has a tense, swollen stomach.
- The dog collapses, loses consciousness or fits.
- The dog vomits several times, and especially if vomiting persists for more than 12 hours.
- The dog suffers from diarrhea for 24 hours or longer.
- The dog's feces are bloodstained.

If in doubt about a particular incident, take your dog to the vet. It's better to be slightly embarrassed about being overly cautious than to lose a pet for not being cautious enough.

Emergency Scenarios

What to do if your dog stops breathing

If your dog has stopped breathing you should give her artificial respiration. The three steps to artificial respiration are:

1. Wrap your hand around your pet's muzzle to seal her lips.

2. Blow into her nose with two quick breaths then give 15-20 breathes per minute. As you breathe you should see her chest rise.

3. Continue until the dog starts to breathe on her own again or you reach medical help.

What to do if your dog is vomiting or dry-retching

If your dog is dry-retching

Dry-retching may be a sign of canine bloat. The dog may manage to puke some debris, but generally there will be no vomit.

Bloat may occur 1–2 hours after eating. Canine bloat is the overstretching of the stomach by gases; the stomach can become twisted as a result. The dog may also show signs of:

- Distress or pain (hunching over).
- Excess salivation.
- Restlessness, panting, whining, drooling.
- Dark red gums (early stage) or pale blue gums (late stage).

Bloat can be fatal so take your dog to the vet immediately.

If your dog is vomiting

It's normal for dogs to vomit occasionally; they often will vomit after eating grass. Grass eating is normal and is a way to settle an upset stomach or aid digestion.

A dog can vomit as a result of a change of diet as some dog's stomachs are sensitive to changes.

Typically what causes an upset stomach when there are diet changes is a change in the protein or carbohydrate in the dog's food or treat. This could be a change from beef to chicken, corn to potato, or simply a different makeup and distribution of ingredients. Most dogs do well with 12–24 hours of fasting after a sudden bout of nausea. This fasting should be followed by slowly reintroducing the normal diet in small amounts for a day or two. Keep in mind that this applies to otherwise healthy pets that aren't showing signs of discomfort, lethargy or dehydration.

If your dog vomits several times – especially if it persists for more than 12 hours – or is experiencing other serious symptoms (see the section above called 'Obvious Signs Your Dog Needs Veterinary Attention'), then take your dog to the vet.

What to do if your dog suffers an allergic reaction

If your dog appears to be suffering an allergic reaction, use antihistamines, prescribed by your vet. Talk to your vet about correct dosage, as this will depend on your dog's weight and other factors. (Make sure the formula does not contain pseudoephedrine.) Watch for a severe reaction such as difficulty breathing which will require an immediate vet visit. Talk to your vet about the possibility of mega-dosing of antihistamines and what amounts are recommended should mega-dosing be required.

What to do if your dog is bitten by a snake

Whilst the US and Australia have a number of poisonous snakes, Britain's only poisonous snake is the Adder, which rarely attacks. Snakebites often occur on the dog's face, head or neck, because dogs use their nose to investigate other animals. However, bites to other areas can also occur.

If your dog:

- has been in a fight with a snake; or
- has been bitten by a venomous snake; or
- has been bitten by a non-venomous snake; or
- suffers sudden facial swelling during a walk or in a snake prone areathen take the following action:

1. Check for difficulty breathing (as a result of shock or swelling in the nasal passage or wind pipe). Apply artificial respiration if your dog stops breathing (see above). Coral snake venom and some rattlesnake venom can paralyze a dog's respiratory system.
2. If available, use the vacuum pump that comes with commercial snakebite kits to remove up to 30% of the venom without an incision (when used within 3 minutes of the bite).
3. Keep your dog still and calm. Keep the dog's activity to a minimum (if you're out on a walk, carry the dog; if she's too big, walk swiftly but don't run). Transport the dog to the vet in a carrier, if you can.
4. Rinse the affected area. Do not cut or poke the area as this may assist the spreading of the venom or otherwise damage surrounding tissue.
5. Remove any paraphernalia such as a harness, collar or clothing so that the dog's breathing is not further restricted if swelling occurs.
6. Keep the dog cool by turning on the air-conditioning in the car – coolness slows circulation. You can also apply a cold pack or other cold item (such as a pack of frozen vegetables) to the area. A pack should only be applied for 10-30 minutes. A cold pack's effect is three-fold: it reduces swelling, reduces pain and slows circulation.
7. Keep the bitten area below the heart's level. This reduces the circulation of the venom.

8. If medical help is more than 1 hour away, then tightly (the same as you would a person had they been bitten) bandage the bite area (if on a leg or the tail) to slow the spread of poison. Do not use a tourniquet.

Aftercare

Death from a venomous snakebite usually occurs within 1 – 2 hours of the bite. The prognosis for dogs who survive beyond that point is good, but the recovery period can last at least ten days.

Snakebites need antibiotics to fight possible infection from bacteria found in snakes' mouths. Your veterinarian may give tetanus and antibiotic injections, and may prescribe antibiotic, anti-inflammatory and painkiller medication. These will help stave off tissue damage and reduce pain.

Snakebite prevention

Treating snakebite can be a really expensive exercise and can cost anywhere in the vicinity of $USD500 to $USD3000. Faced with such an expense, many owners make the awful decision to euthanize their dog. Make sure any pet insurance you take covers snakebites so you never have to face that decision; for more information on pet insurance seeChapter 8: Things You Can Do to Help Your Precious Pup Live a Long & Healthy Life.

There are also three things you can do to help prevent the likelihood of snakebite:

1. Avoid areas where snakes reside, particularly in weedy areas. Snakes are most active at 77°F–90°F (25°C–32°C). As summer approaches avoid night walks as snakes tend to become more nocturnal during these times. If walking at night, remain alert and use a flashlight.
2. Snakes are usually afraid of humans and large animals, so they tend to avoid contact. Thus many snakebites occur because a dog

has flushed an otherwise hidden snake. So, a good precaution is to keep your dog on a leash.

3. Consider 'Snake Avoidance' training. This type of training is offered by dog trainers and is increasing in popularity. The training usually involves using an electronic collar to administer 'shocks' to the dog as she approaches a snake, the objective being that the dog comes to avoid snakes. This is definitely not a type of training that you should try to do yourself as it takes some skill and experience to ensure the process is effective. Make sure any service you consider utilizes a trained and experienced instructor, as only a professional will be able to administer the shocks responsibly. Also ask questions to ensure the snake used in training is treated humanely and according to the prevailing animal protection laws.

What to do if your dog has been in a fight, injured or bleeding

Animal fights

Fights with cats or other dogs may not be as serious as a snakebite, however your dog may suffer punctures that are hard to detect. After a fight, check every part of your dog for wounds, especially puncture wounds, using both your hands and eyes. If you think your dog may have been bitten, contact your vet. You may be able to ask for antibiotic prescription to stem possible infection. Prior to that, cleanse any wounds with antiseptic lotions.

If you don't see any wounds, it's best to monitor your dog for a few days after a fight anyway. If you see signs of lethargy or pain, then a visit to the vet may be needed.

Profuse bleeding

If your dog is bleeding profusely, urgent veterinary attention is needed. In the meantime, you should take immediate steps to stem the bleeding.

Apply a pressure to the wound with a sanitary napkin or large wad of cotton wool. Do not use a tourniquet.

Bandaging a paw or leg

Here are six steps to bandaging a paw or leg:

1. Clean the wound.

2. Place some padding between the dog's toes and over the wound.

3. Wind a bandage over the wound, and above and below the wound, ensuring that the bandage is firm but not so tight as to restrict circulation.

4. Whether it is the leg or paw that is wounded, ensure the bandage includes the dog's paw.

5. Tie the bandage off well above the site of the wound.

6. Cover the bandage with adhesive dressing, firmly but not tightly, and secure it to the back of the dog's leg.

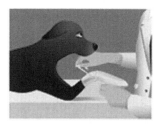

Bandaging an ear

Here are six steps to bandaging a bleeding ear:

1. Clean the wound.
2. Place some padding over the wound on the dog's ear.
3. Fold back the dog's ear and place another pad over (but not inside) the ear's opening.
4. Bandage the ear by starting at the base of the dog's neck and work forward. Enclose the wounded ear.
5. Ensure the unaffected ear is not included in the bandage.
6. Secure the bandage firmly but not so tightlythat it places too much pressure on the dog's neck.

Bandaging a tail

Here are four steps to bandaging a tail:

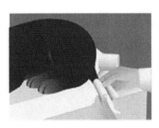 

1. Place a bandage along the length of the tail, making sure you also cover the wound.
2. Lay bandage strips lengthways along the tail.
3. Bandage the tail by encircling it section by section.
4. The bandage should then be covered in adhesive dressing, which should extend beyond the bandage.

What to do if your dog has been run over by a vehicle

A dog that has been hit by a car or another vehicle will require urgent medical attention. Here are nine steps to handling this emergency:

1. Ensure the area where the accident took place is marked well so that traffic does not enter the immediate area, as this can lead to further injury to the dog, first aiders and bystanders. You may have to remove the dog from the area to avoid oncoming traffic. A makeshift stretcher can be made out of clothing or blankets, place the dog gently onto this 'stretcher'. If on your own, lay the 'stretcher' along the dog's back and drag the dog onto it using your hands to support the dog's neck and hips.

2. Ensure the dog is contained by using a leash or makeshift noose. Place this over the dog's head without moving the dog.

3. Improvise a muzzle with a bandage, tie or scarf. A muzzle can be made by placing a bandage over the bridge of the dog's nose, then looping the ends under the dog's chin. Then take the bandage behind the dog's ears and tie firmly on the back of the dog's head. The tie should be tight, but not choke the dog. This should be done before you examine or move the dog, as a distressed dog may bite.

4. Bind any wounds that are bleeding heavily.

5. Have a bystander call the nearest vet to advise of the incoming emergency.

6. Try not to disturb or startle the dog. However, moving the dog may be necessary to obtain medical attention. If so, use the makeshift stretcher to do so. If this cannot be achieved then carry the dog, allowing for any injured limbs to hang free.

7. Do not handle any injured limbs.

8. Do not try to resuscitate an unconscious dog.

9. Take the dog to the nearest vet.

What to do if your dog is choking

Only remove an object from a dog's mouth if you can see it. Never try to remove an object you cannot see from a dog's throat, as this may cause more damage.

You can perform a Heimlich maneuver – an action which may help the dog eject the stuck object – on your dog in three easy steps:

1. Stand behind your dog and steady her.
2. Make a fist.
3. Thrust upwards on the belly below the ribcage.

What to do if your dog is suffering heat stroke or heat exhaustion

Heat stroke can be avoided by providing shade, fresh water and a cool retreat for the dog. Leaving a dog inside a car at any time of year (especially during summer) can have fatal consequences as the temperature inside a car can very quickly reach intolerable levels for a dog. Short-nosed breeds like Chow Chows and Bulldogs are particularly susceptible to over-heating.

Symptoms of heat stroke include distress, panting and/or a blue and swollen tongue. The dog's breathing will be shallow and may be accompanied by throaty noises.

In such cases, the dog needs to be cooled down immediately. Here are three things you can do to cool down your dog:

- Douse your dog, or sponge her, with cold water, paying particular attention to the dog's head.
- Immerse your dog in a cold bath.
- Place a wet towel over your dog's torso, changing it frequently.

After your dog starts to show signs of easier breathing, take her to the vet.

What to do if your dog has been poisoned

Poisoning can occur due to a dog eating, inhaling or absorbing poison through the skin via contact. Since there are many types of poisons, there can be a wide variety of symptoms (most of which will manifest within 3 days). Symptoms of poisoning can include:

- Mouth or skin irritation.
- Glassy eyes.
- Listlessness.
- Vomiting.
- Diarrhea.
- Loss of appetite.
- Drooling or frothing at the mouth.
- Staggering or a 'drunken walk'.
- Over-reaction to sound or light.
- Labored breathing.
- Muscle tremor and rigidity.
- Seizures.
- Collapse.

If you suspect that your dog has consumed something poisonous then you need to seek veterinary help immediately! Talk to your vet's office before trying to induce vomiting. There are cases where inducing vomiting will make things much worse, especially if your dog has ingested something caustic.

Do not make the dog vomit if the poison has already been absorbed into the dog's system – this occurs within approximately 30 minutes of being it being taken.

If your vet recommends that you induce vomiting, choose one of three methods:

1. Give 1–2 teaspoons of 3% hydrogen peroxide every 15 minutes until the dog purges.
2. Give a single dose of 2–3 teaspoons of Syrup of Ipecac.
3. Place two washing soda crystals on the back of the dog's tongue, then make her swallow them by holding your dog's mouth shut and rubbing her throat.

The American Society for the Prevention of Cruelty to Animals (ASPCA) maintains a hotline (1-888-426-4435) which dog owners in the United States can call if they have any queries about suspected poisoning.

What is poisonous to dogs?

- There are a number of plants and flowers that are poisonous to dogs. These include sago palms, rhododendrons, azaleas, lilies of the valley, oleanders, rosebays, foxgloves and kalanchoes. Tulip and daffodil bulbs are also dangerous for dogs. For a more complete listing of garden plants that are toxic to dogs, cats and horses, go to http://www.aspca.org/pet-care/poison-control/plants/. They list 445 plants.
- Cocoa mulch is dangerous to dogs because of its close kinship to chocolate, which is harmful to dogs. Many dogs like to eat cocoa mulch, so please don't use it in your garden.

- Herbicides, insecticides and fertilizers all contains chemicals in one form or another. Even if you are simply using compost, it's likely to contain things that you don't want your dog to ingest. If you are using herbicides or insecticides, be sure to read the labels. Buy brands that say they are safe to use around pets. Most herbicides and insecticides will state how long you need to keep pets away from the area after using. Keep your pets away from the places where you have used herbicides, insecticides, and fertilizers until after the areas are properly dry so your dogs won't be tempted to lick them or pick these wet materials up on their paws.
- If you do keep a compost pile then make sure it's not accessible to your dog.
- If you are using snail pellets or any kind of bait to kill bugs or slugs, make sure that you are using them in a place inaccessible to your dog as they could be harmful to her.
- Toads can be toxic, with exotic toads being more venomous.
- One of the biggest dangers to dogs is (human) prescription medications. Lots of people leave medicine lying around within easy reach of their dogs. Even a small dose of some medicines can be deadly. Acetaminophen, anti-depressants, diet pills, other pain killers and even vitamins can all be very dangerous to your dog. Make sure that you put all medicine up in cabinets where your dog can't access them. If you keep medicine in your purse, make sure you put your purse up where your dog can't reach that either. Dogs often get into people's purses.
- Household cleaners can kill dogs. That's right: common, ordinary, everyday cleaners, like bleach, ammonia and pine cleaners can be toxic to your dog. Don't think your dog will avoid them either. A dog will happily lick bleach just to see what it tastes like.
- Anti-freeze contains ethylene glycol which is poisonous to your dog, yet it has a sweet taste that dogs love. Do not keep this product in your home or sitting out where your dog can reach it. Ice melting products can also be very dangerous to your dog.

- There are many common dangers in our homes that will harm a dog. These include aluminum foil, batteries, coins, moth balls, liquid potpourri, and things that your dog can pick up and eat which may cause an intestinal blockage.
- You should also be aware that some common foods, likely already in your home, are poisonous to dogs. These include raisins and grapes, onions and garlic, macadamia nuts, chocolate and caffeine, and mushrooms.
- Gum is another common household toxin for dogs due to the artificial sweetener used in it called Xylitol. This is also the same chemical found in toothpaste. Both gum and toothpaste can kill your dog.
- Rat and mouse poison is a common household toxin. Unfortunately, many people put out poison for rats without realizing that it will also poison their dog, or, if the dog eats the dead rat, that will poison her. If you have a dog do notuse rat poison at your house. It is deadly.
- Apricot and peach pits can be deadly to dogs. When chewed they release cyanide, and they can cause intestinal blockages.
- Unless you have consulted with your vet first, never give your dog over-the-counter medication for aches and pains including Tylenol, aspirin,ibuprofen, Aleve and other Non-Steroid Anti-inflammatory drug (NSAIDs). These medications can kill your dog.
- Be careful during the holiday period. Poinsettias and Easter lilies can be poisonous to pets. Don't allow your pet to ingest other holiday items such as garlands, ornaments, Christmas tree hooks, small lights, wrapping paper or any other decorations. Dogs have a way of getting into decorations and other materials, often unnoticed, and they can lead to harm.

What to do if your dog has eaten chocolate

Although chocolate in small quantities is not harmful, as a precaution dogs should never be given any chocolate. Why? Have you noticed that people have a hard time eating just one potato chip? Well, the same goes for dogs and chocolate – one taste and they will want (and seek out) more.

Although you probably do not give your dog chocolate, accidents do occur. If your dog has eaten chocolate, the following information will help you decide what to do about it:

1. Determine if the amount of chocolate your dog has eaten is harmful. There are two main factors that will determine whether the dog will have a toxic reaction to chocolate: (a) the concentration of theobromine in the chocolate compared to the dog's weight; and (b) her individual dog's age and health.

   The concentration of theobromine compared to the dog's weight

   Theobromine is a substance found in chocolate which is poisonous to dogs. Milk chocolate and white chocolate have a smaller concentration of theobromine and are therefore less toxic than dark or cooking chocolate. Here's a guide to each type of chocolate:

   • White chocolate: it takes 250 pounds (113 kilograms) of white chocolate to poison a 20 pound (9 kilogram) dog.
   • Milk or semi-sweet chocolate: approximately 1 pound (0.5 kg) of milk chocolate is poisonous to a 20 pound (9 kilogram) dog. As an example, it would take about 2 or 3 chocolate/candy bars to poison a 10 pound (5 kilogram) dog.
   • Dark chocolate or cooking/baking chocolate: just 2 ounces (57 grams) of dark or cooking/bakingchocolate is poisonous to a 20 pound (9 kilogram) dog.

   The dog's age and health

   If the dog is aged or not at optimum health, her tolerance to chocolate may be lowered.

2. See if your dog is exhibiting the following symptoms – if your dog has eaten a toxic amount of chocolate, she will show the

following symptoms within the first two hours: vomiting, diarrhea or hyperactivity. The symptoms will then progress to increased heart rate, arrhythmia, restlessness, muscle twitching, increased urination or excessive panting. More dire symptoms include hyperthermia, muscle tremors, seizures, coma and, ultimately, death.

3. Treat Your Dog. There are three steps in the first aid treatment of chocolate poisoning:

Induce vomiting

In order to do this you can give 1–2 teaspoons of 3% hydrogen peroxide every 15 minutes until the dog purges. Or, give her a single dose of 2–3 teaspoons of Syrup of Ipecac.

Administer an absorption agent

Once vomiting has been induced, it is important to immediately reduce the absorption of theobromine in the dog's stomach. The best way to do this is toadminister activated charcoal mixed with water. The dose is 1 teaspoon for dogs less than 25 pounds (11.3 kilograms) and 2 teaspoons for dogs weighing more than 25 pounds (11.3 kilograms). Use a syringe to administer the dose.

Consult your vet

Advise your vet of the following details:

(i) how much chocolate the dog has eaten
(ii) what type of chocolate
(iii) how long ago the dog ate the chocolate
(iv) the symptoms she is experiencing
(v) the age and general health of your dog
(vi) any first aid you have given her.

Health Hazards in Winter

Winter months – especially in areas where snow and ice are common – can be very hard on dogs, whether they live indoors or outdoors. Here are some tips for caring for your dog during winter:

Indoors

Most people think if their dog lives indoors that they are protected from the worst of winter but even indoor dogs have to go outside. Small dogs and toy dogs, especially, can suffer during winter months.

If you walk your dog on cold sidewalks you may want to consider getting your dog some dog booties. Booties not only keep your dog's paws warm but they will protect her paws from the de-icing chemicals used on sidewalks. These chemicals can be very harmful to a dog's paws, causing them to crack. When a dog licks these chemicals off her paws the chemicals can also be dangerous when ingested.

You can use petroleum jelly to help prevent your dog's paws from cracking.

Small dogs and toy dogs may also need a coat or sweater when they go outdoors during winter. They have less body mass to keep them warm. Dog clothing provides some insulation and heat.

If you have a long-haired dog who ventures outdoors during winter months, be sure to check her paws and long hair when she comes back inside. Ice and snow tends to accumulate on long hair, particularly between a dog's toe pads. Be sure to remove this ice so it won't hurt your dog.

Outdoors

If your dog lives outdoors during the winter you will need to provide your dog with a warm, snug dog house. There are some good dog houses that have a heating element inside to keep your dog warm.

You may wish to provide your dog with a warm dog mat, too.

Be sure that you check your dog's water frequently since cold weather may cause it to freeze. There are waterers that incorporate heating elements to keep them thawed in even the coldest weather. Remember that snow is not a substitute for water.

During very cold temperatures consider bringing your dog into the house.

Remember that wind chill makes the temperature outdoors feel colder than what the thermometer indicates. Your dog will get colder than you think. Try to limit your dog's time outside. Dogs can get frostbite if they are left outdoors too long in freezing conditions.

Be careful if you take your dog near frozen ponds or lakes. These bodies of water sometimes aren't frozen as solid as they seem and it can be easy for a dog to fall through.

Do keep your dog groomed during winter months. Grooming helps keep your dog well-insulated which will keep her warmer.

Make sure you feed your dog some extra calories in the winter, especially if she lives outside. Your dog needs the extra calories to keep herself warm.

If your dog gets wet from rain or snow it's a good idea to use a blow dryer to dry her off. This will help her warm up faster.

Don't leave your dog alone in a car in the winter, even with the engine running. Carbon monoxide can kill your dog.

Each season has its hazards for dogs and winter is no exception. Watch out for these weather-related issues and you can keep your dog warm and safe during winter.

Your Dog's First-Aid Kit

You can store your dog's first-aid essentials with your family's first-aid kit, however it's best to ensure they are kept in a separate, labeled and water proof container so there's no possibility of mixing contents. Make sure it is out of reach of both children and pets. If you use the services of a pet sitter, remember to let this person know where the dog's first-aid kit is located.

Make a periodic inventory of the first-aid kit to ensure that the items in it have not expired or have gone missing.

When you are putting your kit together, ask your vet for any suggestions in relation to your dog's breed and age, and your own lifestyle.

Here is a list of supplies which should be included in a dog's first-aid kit:

- A card detailing your vet's name, location and contact number. The location of the nearest animal hospital, animal ambulance and poison hotline.
- Pet insurance details and contact numbers.
- An inventory of items and expiry dates.
- Bandages.
- Vet wrap: a great adhesive which is not overly sticky to fur.
- Absorbent cotton wool.
- Gauze bandages (5cm/2in and 10cm/4in) and adhesive tape.
- Gauze swabs.
- Cotton buds.
- Sanitary napkins: good for wounds that are bleeding profusely.
- Bottle of hydrogen peroxide.
- Mineral oil (which works well as a laxative).
- Anti-bacterial ointment cream (helps prevent infections and seals wounds). You may also want to keep eye ointments handy, but do not use them if there is a foreign object in the eye.
- Antibiotic or antiseptic ointment (like Betadine).
- Eyewash or eye drops (helps to wash away debris or dirt that may worsen eye injuries).
- Cleansing ear drops.
- Rectal or ear thermometer.
- Plastic syringe (½ fl oz; 20ml): good for administering liquid medications. They should not be used to squirt any liquid directly into the ear canal.

- Rescue cream: good for bruises, cuts, abrasions, flaky skin.
- Activated charcoal: estimated to reduce the absorption of poisonous substances by up to 60%. Syrup of Ipecac and 3% hydrogen peroxide are also good for reducing the absorption of poison. Washing soda is also effective in inducing vomiting.
- Bismuth: helps to settle upset stomachs and can be used for diarrhea, nausea and motion sickness.
- Scissors with a blunt end, used for cutting bandages, tape or matted hair. Scissors are also good for trimming hair around wounds.
- Cold compress.
- Tweezers and a tick removal tool. Tweezers or forceps are useful for removing splinters from paws and faces. Forceps, which should not be used as a probe in any injury as this may worsen it.
- Pain reliever. Contact your vet for advice on the best type and doses of human medication. Remember that some human pain medication is potentially harmful for dogs (and cats). Aspirin (given with food) can be used for mild pain, but only in very small doses – check with your vet about the right dose for your dog. A dog cannot digest enteric-coated aspirin. Ibuprofen can be toxic. Never give a medication prescribed for another person or pet to your dog.
- Antihistamines are good for allergies, insect bites and itching. Make sure the formula does not contain pseudoephedrine.
- A large blanket to keep your dog warm and help to stave off shock.
- A soft muzzle is a good idea, because even a good natured dog may bite when in pain or shock.
- Electrolyte fluids can help rehydrate a dog if she is suffering from chronic vomiting or diarrhea.
- Herbal remedies and supplements may be useful, but check with your vet to ensure they do not react badly with other medications.
- Commercial snakebite kit (if you live in a country with poisonous snakes), including a vacuum.
- A first aid book for dogs.

Dog Essentials for Your Evacuation Kit

Many families have an emergency or evacuation kit stocked with essentials like food, water and other items to help through a relocation as a result of fire, flood or other natural disaster. When stocking your evacuation kit, remember to include a first-aid kit for your dog as well as the following items:

Water and food

Make sure there is enough dried and canned food for your dog for two weeks. You should check expiration dates on the food labels and replace water every couple of months. Make sure you have a can-opener and spoons in the kit too! Your kit should also have a small portable water bowl made of soft material (these can be purchased at camping stores) and food bowls. Include your dog's favorite treats too.

Essential equipment

Make sure you have also packed the following items for your dog in your evacuation kit:

- Muzzle (frightened dogs may bite) - you can buy either a soft or hard muzzle from most pet stores.
- Bitter Apple or other product that discourages licking (some dogs do this when nervous).
- Pet carrier.
- Spare lead and collar (with a tag that has your contact details).
- A blanket/thermal blanket and some toys.
- Poo bags/plastic bags and disinfectant.
- Grooming, dental cleaning supplies and soap.

Essential papers

Your kit should have two copies of the following papers:

- Updated vaccination certificate.
- Pet insurance details and policy number.
- Microchip/tattoo ID and documentation.
- Photos of you with your dog. Write your dog's name and your contact details on the back of the photos. (Make sure the contact details of a friend or relative are also recorded on the back of the photos, in case you cannot be reached).
- Proof of ownership, such as registration, purchase or adoption papers.

You should also have a list of the contact details for the following places:

- Your vet and any secondary vets.
- Nearest emergency animal hospitals, clinics or poison centers (which may be required if your dog becomes ill or injured).
- Animal shelters, pet friendly motels, boarding facilities, microchip/tattoo ID centers. These numbers are good to have if you are either looking to find accommodation for your pet or if you are in the unfortunate position of looking for your dog.

One copy of these papers and the list of contact details can be placed in the evacuation kit with your other personal papers (in a zip lock bag or container). The second set of papers can be placed in a zip lock bag and taped to the inside wall of the pet carrier. Make a note with indelible ink on the outside of the carrier that there is important information about the dog and owner within. This is an especially useful measure if you want to make it easier to reclaim your dog, should you become separated.

Medication

The evacuation kit should have a supply of any medication your dog takes regularly, including monthly doses of heartworm/intestinal worm/ flea preventatives. Keep these medications dry in waterproof containers.

Should your dog be prone to anxiety as a result of changes in routine or bad weather (such as storms), ask your vet about any remedies that may be worth storing in your evacuation kit.

Saying Goodbye – Dealing with Death

As your dog ages the time may come when you begin to wonder if she still has the same quality of life she had when she was younger. Is she eating well? Does she still have good mobility? Does she have chronic pain? Does she have any kind of veterinary medical condition which is worsening or which is causing her to suffer or lose interest in life? These are all issues that may cause you to consider euthanasia for your dog.

Euthanasia - When is the best time?

It is always hard to say when it is the best time to let your beloved pet go and it is never easy to say goodbye. If your dog has a difficult veterinary condition and she is suffering or in pain, then you should think carefully about releasing her from suffering. Your veterinarian can often advise you in these situations. In some cases your dog may require extensive veterinary care without a guarantee of improvement. This is another situation where you may need to make the difficult decision to release your friend.

In some cases the cost of care may be a factor. The cost of veterinary care is often on a par with human medicine now. Veterinarians can offer MRIs, chemotherapy, prosthetic limbs, advanced surgical techniques and many other treatments. However, the cost of these treatments may be prohibitive for most pet owners – which is why pet insurance is so important.

There may be some cases where you need to put a healthy dog to sleep. This may happen if your dog is having problems with temperament, being aggressive, or if she has been deemed dangerous. It is very hard to say goodbye to a young, healthy dog, for whatever reason.

If you decide that it is time to say goodbye to your pet, you will most likely take her to the vet's office. However, in some cases, particularly with very old pets, the veterinarian may come to your home. This is usually a very difficult time for the owner and you will probably want a friend or family member to be with you. The veterinarian will often give your pet a tranquilizer first, to help relax her. Then the vet will give your pet a drug to induce euthanasia by helping your pet become unconscious. Your pet will drift off and it will be painless and gentle. Your pet will feel just like she is falling asleep.

It is never easy to say goodbye to your pet but it's something that we all must do at some point. We should offer our pets the best care possible but when we have provided all the care we are able to give, we should give them a dignified release.

Celebrating the life of your pet

When celebrating the life of your dog, you may like to consider the following perspective of Sophia Cull, celebrant and founder of 'The Vow Exchange':

For many people, the 'family pet' is more family than pet. Children who are either born into a family with a pet, or who welcome a pet into their home when very young, may not know life without that dog! Therefore, when the pet passes away, it may be the child or teenager's first experience of death.

Taking into consideration all the variables you may face, celebrating the life of your pet with a funeral is still possible. A funeral can provide a ritual of farewell and completion for your family. While children's understanding of death changes as they grow, we shouldn't underestimate the adult who fed, washed, walked, trained and if required gave medication to that animal, possibly for many years – everyone has their own process of grieving.

Some family members may not be able to participate in a funeral ceremony due to their own beliefs or desires. It is important not to 'force' family members to participate if that is not their thing. Everyone has his own beliefs. If your family is split on this issue, just hold one for those who are interested and the others may join in later or not at all. Grief is an individual journey and it is important that we allow people their own beliefs.

If your family is just you and your pets, it is also important to do what is right for you. Having a friend participate in the funeral with you can make it easier. If your friend knows you well enough they should not be surprised by your invitation to stand with them at this moment.

Should you want to hold your own pet funeral there are some simple ways you can do this. Firstly you may want to consider some symbolic rituals. These can include but not limited to:

1. Creating a coffin/box or special bag tailor made for your pet and painted or decorated as appropriate for the pet and family members' needs. (Your perspective on environmental sustainability may affect your choices here).
2. Including items specific to the pet such as a blanket, toy, collar or registration tags.
3. Planting a tree in their memory or having a dedicated pot plant.
4. Framing a photo of your pet or a collage of photos with the family.
5. Having a special candle to light for the ceremony and thereafter if required (there are many ways you can decorate the candle if you are craftily inclined).

The ceremony itself can be tailored to meet your needs. A basic structure may include:

1. Introduction – a brief declaration of why you have gathered at this moment.
2. An eulogy or story telling session about the pet and their life with your family– one or more family members might what to

recall a story about the pet that illustrates their characteristics or something funny/important/clever/unique that they did.
3. If you choose you may have a reading, a poem or a prayer.
4. Any rituals you would like to include.
5. Wishes – for instance if the dog had been unwell before passing away, the wish may center on the fact that she is no longer in pain. In addition you may want to make a wish for the family, such as that they will find comfort in their memories.
6. Closing – a conclusion that ties it all together and ends on a happy note.

The question "how soon after can we get the next pet?" is often asked. It is often suggested that a short time between pets be observed. How short or long a time you leave will vary between people and families. It is also important to consider other pets you have and the impact a new animal might have on them.

A celebration of the life of your pet can give everyone a memorable closure to a life well lived.

Resources

Bailey, Gwen. "What is My Dog Doing That? Understanding Your Pet's Puzzling Behaviour." Octopus Publishing Group, 2009.

Larkin, Dr. Peter. "How to Look After Your Dog: An Expert Practical Guide to Dog Care, Grooming, Feeding and First Aid." Anness Publishing Ltd, 2008.

Lindsay, Steven R. "Handbook of Applied Dog Behavior and Training: Volume One - Adaption and Learning." Blackwell Publishing, 2000.

Lindsay, Steven R. "Handbook of Applied Dog Behavior and Training: Volume Two – Etiology and Assessment of Behavior Problems." Blackwell Publishing, 2001.

MacDonald, Carina. "Dog Care & Training: A Complete Illustrated Guide to Adopting, House-Breaking, and Raising a Healthy Dog." Morris Book Publishing, 2009.

Messent, Peter. "Understanding Your Dog." A.P. Publishing Pty Ltd, 1979.

Reid, Pamela J. "Excel-erated Learning: Explaining How Dogs Learn and Best to Teach Them in Plain English." James & Kenneth Publishers, 1996.

Rogers, Tammie. "4-H Guide Dog Training & Dog Tricks." Voyageur Press, 2009.

Volhard, Jack & Wendy. "Dog Training for Dummies." Wiley Publishing, 2005.

Wilson, Sylvia. "The Bark Busters Guide to Dog Behaviour and Training." Simon & Schuster, 2003.

Made in the USA
San Bernardino, CA
02 January 2013